D1375137

WAR

Please renew or return items by the date shown on your receipt

www.hertsdirect.org/libraries

Renewals and enquiries:

0300 123 4049

Textphone for hearing or speech impaired

0300 123 4041

Hertfordshire

521 286 48 1

THE ESSENTIAL GUIDE TO
PSYCHIC POWERS

DEVELOP YOUR INTUITIVE, TELEPATHIC AND HEALING SKILLS

SARAH BARTLETT

WATKINS PUBLISHING
LONDON

The Essential Guide to Psychic Powers
Sarah Bartlett

First published in the UK and USA in 2012 by
Watkins Publishing, an imprint of Duncan Baird
Publishers Ltd
Sixth Floor, Castle House
75–76 Wells Street
London W1T 3QH

Conceived, created and designed by Duncan
Baird Publishers

Managing Editor: Sandra Rigby
Produced by Bookworx: **Editor** Jo Godfrey
Wood; **Designer** Peggy Sadler
Picture Research: Emma Copestake
and Bookworx

British Library Cataloguing-in-Publication Data:
A CIP record for this book is available from the
British Library
Library of Congress Cataloging-in-Publication
Data available

ISBN: 978-1-78028-113-1

10 9 8 7 6 5 4 3 2 1

Typeset in Myriad Pro
Colour reproduction by XY Digital
Limited, London
Printed in China by Imago

Notes:
Abbreviations used throughout this book:
CE Common Era (the equivalent of AD)
BCE Before the Common Era (the
equivalent of BC)

Distributed in the USA and Canada by
Sterling Publishing Co., Inc.
387 Park Avenue South
New York, NY 10016-8810

For information about custom editions,
special sales, premium and corporate
purchases, please contact Sterling Special
Sales Department at 800-805-5489 or
specialsales@sterlingpub.com.

Contents

Introduction

Psyche is an ancient Greek word, meaning "soul" or "invisible animating spirit", and the word "psychic", therefore, means "of the soul". This internal essence of ourselves, an interface between the invisible universal flow of energy and the manifest world, is the key to unlocking the secrets of other dimensions.

Whether you're a beginner, longing to discover or develop your psychic powers, or want to go one step further to increase your clairvoyant or divination skills, this book will give you all the information you need.

But what is the soul?

The soul is the invisible or ethereal part of ourselves that exists beyond the physical body. Thought to exist before the body comes into being, it will continue to exist after the body is no more. This "soul essence" connects us with the energy of the universe and with the past, the present and the future. Your psychic sense, often known as the "sixth sense" and "extra-sensory perception" (ESP), interprets the soul's messages from the cosmos in a language we can easily understand.

Psychic power

The world of psychic power has been scorned, mistrusted and feared for thousands of years, largely because it has remained unexplained and therefore appears threatening. But, as with any power, there are always those who try to abuse or corrupt it. In the West, prophecy, scrying and contacting spirits or angels, for example, have all been associated with evil and considered heretical.

If you decide to develop your psychic power, you must do so with utter honesty and the belief that you are acting for the good of everything in the

The belief that there is something more than
the physical world around us is at heart of
most religious and mystical belief systems.
In medieval Europe it was thought that the
canopy of stars of the known cosmos could
be breached. Mankind could discover not
only new worlds, but also, as individuals, at
last be at one with the universe.

A calm environment is required when you are using your psychic powers.

universe. You must also learn to protect yourself from the draining energies of the psychic world and from negative psychic invasion from those around you.

The first chapter (see pages 10–39) explains the power of the mind and its psychic realms, and includes a questionnaire to help you determine how psychic you are (see page 38). The second chapter (see pages 40–85) delves deeper into the different types of psychic power, revealing everything you need to know about your sixth sense, the power of your imagination, preparing yourself for psychic work and the protective measures and precautions you must always take. Chapter 3 (see pages 86–133) teaches you how to use your psychic powers for healing and protection, and Chapter 4 (see pages 134–65) and Chapter 5 (see pages 166–211) give you divination techniques and psychic tools to enhance your own powers and plunge further into the realms beyond so-called reality. Finally, in Chapter 6 (see pages 212–35) and Chapter 7 (see pages 236–71) you can learn about altered states of the mind and the other dimensions of psychic power, such as astral travel, and how to get in touch with your guardian angel.

The gift

Our innate psychic sense gives us access to the soul's hidden knowledge and provides feedback on the state of others as well as ourselves. It also reveals information that would normally be unavailable or hidden. This paranormal ability to perceive things that are not normally recognized by the five senses brings us into contact with other supernatural, or spirit, worlds. Some people remain unaware of this gift, while others ignore it, often finding life difficult because they are sensitive not only to other people but to the invisible realms, too. They have not learned how to protect themselves from psychic invasion. Others readily make use of this energy from childhood and develop their powers or try to rediscover them in adulthood.

Psychic abilities such as intuition and channelling are all a means to reveal hidden information, either from another individual, or, as in the case of channelling, from spirit guides or ascended masters. Other psychic dimensions include working with past lives and out-of-body experiences, as well as telepathy, psychokinesis and psychometry. The power is there within us, waiting to be liberated and nurtured, but it must be used with care.

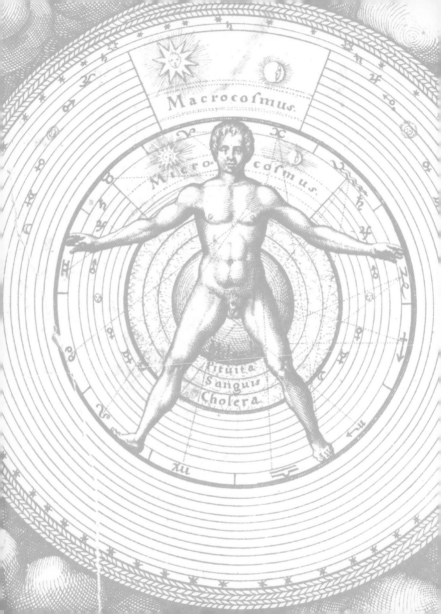

chapter 1

What is psychic power?

Psychic power is the ability to tap into the cosmic energy field flowing through everything, including the supernatural or paranormal planes. Mystics, occultists, sages and Eastern philosophers all believe that cosmic energy is accessible to all of us, at any time.

There are many types of psychic power and this book will help you to develop your own, whether by using your intuition, learning clairvoyance and divining, tapping into the minds of others, becoming a medium to contact spirit guides, travelling the shamanic and astral realms or in out-of-body experiences. Our psychic power is within us at birth, but we may lose this instinct as we grow up in the left-brain-governed world. This power lies dormant; now is the time to wake it up.

Historical background

The word "psychic" is currently used as an umbrella term for a wide range of people with psychic skills, including clairvoyance, telepathy, spiritual channelling or the ability to use psychic tools, such as the Tarot, pendulum-dowsing and other divination techniques.

Some form of psychic perception has been at the core of many religions and spiritual belief systems throughout all the cultures of the world. Astrologers, seers, oracles, prophets and shamans were, and continue to be, considered to possess a mysterious mystical power or an ability to contact the dead or spirits of the dead.

Early explorations into the psychic world

In Ancient Egypt, the snake-headed goddess Wadjet (eye of the moon) was a renowned oracle and this prophetic tradition spread to Ancient Greece, where oracles, usually inspired by messages from the gods, were frequently priestesses. The most famous Greek oracle was the Pythia (see picture, right), who sat in a trance above the narcotic breath-like fumes of the serpent in the ground beneath her. The god Apollo would speak through her, usually in the form of inarticulate messages, which would then be interpreted. And in China, divinatory oracle bones have been found dating back to the Shang Dynasty, 1600BCE, which are very similar to the I Ching system (see pages 200–7).

The predictions of Nostradamus

Michel de Nostredame (1503–1566), the French seer, became notorious for his predictions of war, famine, plagues and the future of European kings. He began his career as an apothecary, but after a visit to Italy became interested in the occult and wrote an almanac for 1550. He changed his name to

The Priestess of Delphi by John Collier (1850–1934) depicts Pythia engulfed in narcotic fumes emerging through a fissure in the rock below.

From the mid-19th century the seance became a hugely popular form of parlour entertainment and many people dabbled in the activity. Seances were used to receive messages directly from spirits or via a medium. They came to be a form of social activity as much as a serious engagement with the spirit world.

"Nostradamus" and, after the success of the first almanac, continued to write one a year. Containing over 6,000 predictions, the almanac's great popularity among the nobility meant that he was soon commissioned to make horoscopes and to give psychic advice. He began work on *The Prophecies*, a collection of prophetic quatrains (stanzas of four lines), most of which seem to be reworkings of sacred texts and extracts from the Neoplatonists and earlier Classical sources. Although Nostradamus is reputed to have predicted some famous events accurately, such as the execution of Charles I of England, there is speculation that his words have been misinterpreted or simply that he manipulated or misquoted obscure language and cryptic texts.

From the end of the 17th century, Christian and other religious beliefs were beginning to be occluded by the Age of Enlightenment and the world of science. A new spirit of scientific enquiry inspired research such as that of German physician Franz Anton Mesmer (1734–1815), who theorized that between every animate and inanimate object there was a spiritual energy he called *magnétisme animal*, later known as "mesmerism". After seeing a performance by Swiss mesmerist, Charles Lafontaine, the Scottish surgeon James Braid developed the concept of "hypnosis" in 1842.

The rise of spiritualism

The main tenet of spiritualist belief is that mediums, or channellers, contact spirits of the dead, giving insight to the living. With the popularity of the controversial New York mediums, the Fox Sisters (see page 249), in the mid-19th century, contacting the dead in seances became a common parlour game and led to renewal of interest in spiritual matters and the development of the spiritualist movement in an age of growing scientific reason. Documenting and discrediting spirit-rappings and other manifestations of spirits were popular activities. However, many spirit messages were found to be accurate or were witnessed by respected individuals, such as Abraham Lincoln and his wife, who attempted to contact their dead son. From the 1850s onward, the paranormal was officially investigated. The Davenport Brothers (see page 16), famed for stage illusions, were exposed as fraudsters by Harry Houdini (1874–1926), the Hungarian-born escapologist. This did little to enhance the reputation of the spiritualist movement, the role of mediums or those with genuine clairvoyant abilities.

The Ghost Club and the Society for Psychical Research

Founded in Cambridge, UK, by a group of Trinity College fellows in 1855, the Ghost Club's members were convinced that psychic phenomena existed. They investigated the Davenport Brothers' "spirit cabinet", although their findings were never made public. Despite its name, members of the Ghost Club were actually more interested in spirits than ghosts (see page 260). The Ghost Club was revived in 1882, in the same year as the founding of Society for Psychical Research (SPR), which concentrated on a more unbiased

William and Ira Davenport were among the many performing mediums and psychics of the mid-19th century who were instrumental in developing the popularity of the American and European spiritualist movements.

scientific method of investigation. The society, which still exists today, was made up of eminent scholars and psychologists such as Edmund Gurney and Frederick Myers, who coined the word "telepathy". Other distinguished members included physicist Sir Oliver Lodge, writers Sir Arthur Conan Doyle and W.B. Yeats.

The 20th century

Max Dessoir, German philosopher and theorist of aesthetics, coined the term "parapsychology" in 1889 and this was adopted in the 1930s by the American psychologist J.B. Rhine in his investigation into extra-sensory

Edgar Cayce was an American psychic healer whose belief in Plato's legendary sunken island of Atlantis helped to promote an interest in psychic archaeology.

perception (ESP) and psychokinesis. Popular psychics of this period include the American Edgar Cayce (1877–1945), who was renowned for trance-healing. According to Cayce, the unconscious mind had access to information the conscious mind did not, and he developed spiritual teachings consisting of an array of themes, including destiny and reincarnation. Cayce also claimed to have the powers to carry out astral projection, mediumship, aura-reading and prophecy.

Today, psychics reach a wide audience through television, newspapers and books and include individuals such as American TV personality Joyce Keller, Brazilian psychic surgeon João de Deus, channellers Jane Roberts and Esther Hicks and mediums such as British Derek Acorah and Tony Stockwell.

The scientific viewpoint and parapsychology

If Eastern traditions recognize universal energy (often called *chi* or *prana*) flowing through and present in all living things, modern physics has, to a certain extent, supported this concept. The great physicist, Albert Einstein (1879–1955) stated not only that all matter consists of energy, but also that space and time are relative rather than absolute. This can help to explain how a psychic individual can see beyond the illusion of time and space. Mystics and quantum physicists seem to be in agreement that cosmic consciousness is immanent, which means that it can be accessed at any moment – if we only know how.

Extra-sensory perception

Much research into extra-sensory perception (ESP), telepathy and intuition was carried out by scientists and psychologists throughout the 20th century. In the 1930s J.B. Rhine and his wife, Louisa, developed psychic research into

Zener cards

J.B. Rhine and psychologist Karl Zener developed a method of testing for extra-sensory perception (ESP) that involved subjects guessing which symbol, out of five possibilities, would appear when going through a deck of cards (see page 83). Decks were specifically designed for this purpose, named "Zener cards" (see page 82). More than a 20 percent correct guess ratio was perceived as higher than mere chance, indicating psychic ability. Rhine stated in his first book, *Extrasensory Perception* (1934), that after 90,000 trials he felt ESP was "an actual and demonstrable occurrence".

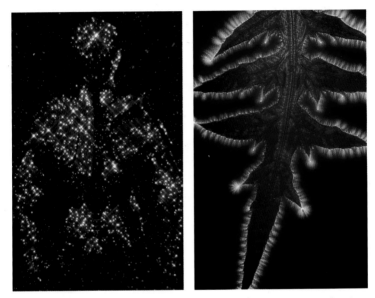

Kirlian photography was discovered and developed by Russian inventor Semyon Kirlian in the 1930s. It is still used today to observe the aura of the human body and other life forms.

a form of experimental psychology. To avoid associations with mediums, ghosts and spirits, they dubbed it "parapsychology". Throughout the 1940s and 1950s, Rhine and other psychologists carried out independent experiments and reported significant results to suggest that ESP was effective, but still could not explain why.

In the 1970s, parapsychology became a popular scientific study. Canadian psychiatrist Ian Stevenson conducted research into reincarnation, while psychologist Thelma Moss studied Kirlian photography, a method said to determine the presence of the aura. The influx of Eastern philosophies and

With the rise of the scientific study of paranormal phenomenon, by the late 1940s investigations, tests and experiments by students in psychology departments across the US and the UK became the norm. This class of 1946 are investigating the powers of telekinesis.

spiritual teachers from Asia, and their claims of abilities produced by meditational states, led to research on altered states of consciousness by American psychologist Dr Charles Tart. The American Society for Psychical Research conducted experiments in out-of-body experiences, while physicist Russell Targ coined the term "remote viewing" in 1974, referring to the ability of an individual to observe any person or object in any part of the world via astral projection. In 1988, the National Academy of Sciences in the US published a report on parapsychology claiming that after a hundred or so years of research there was still no conclusive evidence that such phenomena existed. In the same report, however, they also recommended monitoring psychokinesis using random number generators and to continue research into findings of the Ganzfeld Effect, a phenomenon of visual perception caused by staring at a uniform field of colour.

Experimental support and criticism

Astrophysicist Carl Sagan has also suggested that there are three claims in parapsychology that have at least some experimental support and "deserve serious study". These are: first, the theory

UK physicist and Nobel Prize winner Brian David Josephson is a major proponent of parapsychology today.

that humans can influence random number generators in computers; second, the theory that people under mild sensory deprivation can receive thoughts or images "projected" at them and third, that young children have reported details of a previous life that turn out to be accurate when they could not have known those details in any other way than via reincarnation.

Although in the UK parapsychology is still researched in many university psychology departments, most scientists regard the discipline as a pseudoscience, complaining that its proponents have been unable to show any conclusive evidence of psychic abilities. UK psychologist and one-time magician Richard Wiseman has criticized the parapsychological community for widespread errors in research methods. However, UK physicist Brian David Josephson and other supporters of parapsychology have spoken of "irrational attacks on parapsychology", which stem from the difficulties of "putting these phenomena into our present system of the universe".

How the mind works

Most people think of the "mind" as simply being the brain. We now know a great deal about the brain, thanks to scientific research into its evolution, processes and functions. But what is the mind, exactly? One definition suggests it is the ability to reason and think, via the faculty of consciousness. In fact, many scientists, mystics and psychologists have very different views on what the mind is and what it is not. We need to take a look at some of these theories before we go any further, for the exploration of the mind, which is still ongoing, is as fascinating as the exploration of the universe itself.

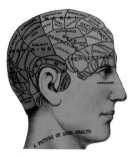

Developed by German physician Franz Joseph Gall in 1796 and popularized in the 19th century, phrenology was the study of specific areas of the brain to determine character and individual perception.

The brain

The brain is complex and made up of three main parts: the forebrain, or cerebrum, the midbrain and hindbrain, or cerebellum. The forebrain, the most recently evolved part of the brain, contains the left and right hemispheres, said to control motor, sensory and cognitive functions, as well as reproductive, emotional, eating and sleeping functions. Scientists have discovered that the left side of the brain is responsible for rational, analytical thought processes, while the right is responsible for abstract thought, non-verbal perception, visual and spatial awareness and intuition. Working in tandem, the two halves of the forebrain complement each other. However some people are more "right-brained" and others more "left-brained" in their approach to life and general behaviour.

Are you more right- or left-brained?

Here's a short test to see whether you have a right- or left-brained tendency. The intuitive and perceptive right brain is the side you need to develop in order to unlock your psychic powers. Answer "Yes" or "No" to each of these statements:

Y N

❑ ❑ I find meaning in symbols, images and experiences.

❑ ❑ Fantasy, fiction and imagination are important to me.

❑ ❑ When I'm lost or confused I trust my "gut" feelings.

❑ ❑ I often lose track of place and time when I'm being creative.

❑ ❑ I don't like carrying out mathematical tasks or making lists.

❑ ❑ I prefer to follow my hunches than listen to reason.

❑ ❑ I often act without thinking.

❑ ❑ Other people tell me I'm psychic.

❑ ❑ I see the "big picture", not just the details.

❑ ❑ I can always remember someone's face, but not always their name.

❑ ❑ I like taking risks.

❑ ❑ My desk looks chaotic, but I know where everything is.

❑ ❑ I often think of someone and then they phone me a moment later.

RESULTS

★ If you agreed with more than seven of the above statements, then your right brain is dominant.

★ If you disagreed with more than seven, your left brain is dominant.

★ If you have more or less equal "yes" and "no" answers, then your left and right brain are fairly evenly balanced.

The nature of the mind

If the mind is not just the brain, then what is it? We know that the mind is concerned with the ability to reason, our intellect, our conscious thought and our will. But the mind also includes our unconscious: our dreams, intuition, creativity, imagination and a wide range of psychic powers, plus the ability to have exceptional human experiences (the umbrella term for altered states of consciousness) and near-death and out-of-body experiences. If the mind is both our consciousness and our unconsciousness, then there are various ways of looking at it (see below), both spiritual and scientific, that can help us to understand what it can and cannot do.

The nature of consciousness

According to the scientific viewpoint, consciousness is an awareness, via our sensory perception, of the external world, as well as of ourselves. In other words, self-awareness is a sign of consciousness. Philosophy takes another viewpoint – that consciousness is our personal awareness of any given moment and that everything that is part of that moment; it is one's conscious experience of both the known and the unknown, of both the familiar and the mysterious.

Some theorists link consciousness to quantum mind theory, or space-time and electromagnetic theories, which explain that the experience of consciousness is not just limited to brain activity. Meanwhile, parapsychologists rely on the currently unmeasurable psychic powers of psychokinesis and telepathy to support the belief that consciousness is not merely confined to the brain.

According to psychologists Sigmund Freud and Carl Jung, the unconscious mind is just as important as the conscious mind. Freud believed that unconscious drives have a profound influence on our lives, but Jung also proposed that the holistic health of an individual must include a spiritual dimension. He believed the unconscious mind was the connection to our spiritual heritage, a link to our soul and also to the soul of the whole world. Jung called this the "collective unconscious". This was likened to a storehouse of archetypes going back millions of years in our human evolution and which we all carry at a deep level within our personal psyches.

Universal energy

Mystics, psychics and spiritual writers of today also believe that universal, or cosmic, energy is linked to our own conscious and unconscious minds. Immanent throughout the universe, this is the energy that binds everything together

Carl Jung and Sigmund Freud, seen here at Clark University in 1909, were pioneers of the exploration of the unconscious.

and which flows through everything. Known as *chi* to the ancient Taoists, this energy is now commonly called "subtle energy".

However, among scientists there is an ongoing debate about the unconscious. Cognitive psychologists, for example, maintain that the unconscious merely consists of those mental processes that are not mediated by any sensory perception.

Working toward mastery of the mind

If the mind is the interaction of both the conscious and unconscious mind, we need to learn to control our conscious mind if we are to tap into the universal energy field, accessed through our unconsciousness. Being the master of your own mind is not always easy – remember that the conscious mind may well have a mind of its own!

As in the Buddhist practice of mindfulness, we need to calm the babblings of our thoughts by using techniques such as meditation and visualization to take an objective view of the busy mind. This part of our consciousness gets into habits, both lazy ones and anxious ones. By knowing that you don't have to accept or listen to the thoughts that run through your head, you begin to realize that you can reject the negative thoughts and flip them into positive ones. This is having mastery of your mind. It is "you" at your very source.

Sometimes this source is called the Higher Self or the Third Eye. It is also the route through which your mind works to move outside itself, to align with soul and access the invisible, or spiritual, world. Psychic powers rely on developing and controlling other parts of the mind and knowing that you are still master of that mind. These include imagination and concentration, will-power, discipline, motivation, self-confidence, detachment and calmness. If you strengthen and develop this part of your mind, you then can work with, and through, the energy fields around you. This is the merging of body and mind with soul and is the pathway to true psychic power.

Meditation is one of the best ways to still the mind, open up to altered states of consciousness and activate your psychic powers.

Subtle energy

Subtle energy is most famously found in Eastern religions, such as Hinduism and Buddhism, but members of the mystic branches of Christianity and Judaism also believe that there are layers of energy (or Life Force) flowing between the inner self of the body and the numinous. Invisible energy is believed to penetrate everything and can be harnessed for healing and developing our psychic consciousness. By tapping into this force field, we can use subtle energy to "psyche out" and heal others and ourselves, find lost objects or communicate with other people or the spiritual world. Unexplained, as yet, by science, subtle energy also refers to the medium through which our consciousness influences both animate and inanimate matter. Still baffled by exactly what this energy is, some scientists think it may be a field of energy beyond the electromagnetic spectrum's gamma rays.

Experiments with subtle energy

Energy researcher Cleve Backster demonstrated how human emotions can affect the cells of plants and vegetables. He also experimented with white blood cells taken from a human donor whose emotions continued to influence the behaviour of the cells, even at a distance. Known as the Backster Effect, this is similar to the "morphogenic field concept" put forward by British biologist Rupert Sheldrake, who theorized that an intention-laden force field is transmitted from one being to another. Sheldrake believed this to be behind the Vedic concept of the Akashic Records, the cosmic "library" of all experiences and memories of human minds from their physical lifetime.

Yale professor Harold Saxton Burr postulated the L-field (life field) as the electromagnetic field of any organism, while colleague Leonard Ravitz took this idea further and investigated the effects of the lunar cycle on the human

Chi gung is said to work with the body's subtle energy system, which pervades all life. The Chinese refer to this energy as *chi*.

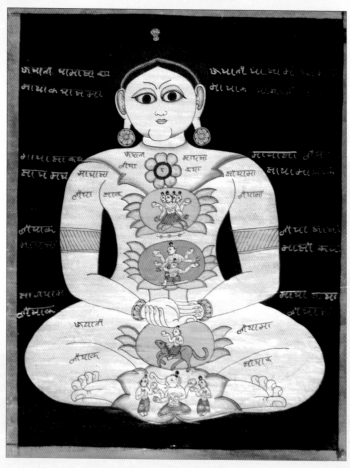

The symbolic representation of the lower chakras, visualized in this traditional Nepalese painting as Hindu gods within lotus-flower shapes.

L-field. He commented that "emotions can be equated with energy", later showing that the L-field disappears as a whole before physical death.

There have been many other theories about subtle energy, known as the "Odic force" by 19th-century Baron Von Reichenbach. The main force behind the auric field discovered in Kirlian photography (see page 19), subtle energy also empowers out-of-body experiences (OBEs), astral projection and altered states of consciousness. Traditional disciplines, such as Feng Shui, Indian yoga, Ayurveda and divination work such as pendulum-dowsing, work with the unseen energy fields that exist between us. We must also learn to create boundaries and prevent energy invasion from individual and collective energy fields. By safely harnessing our innate psychic ability, we can channel and use subtle energy.

The subtle body

The chakra (see pages 94–9) and aura systems are the subtle energy field of the body. They have been described in different ways in various traditions. The word chakra comes from the Sanskrit word for "wheel"; the chakras are considered to be spinning vortices of energy radiating from the body, vibrating independently from the auric field. Our energy field must be balanced and strengthened for well-being and psychic work.

Whereas subtle energy is both outside ourselves and yet flowing through us, the "subtle body" is a phrase used to determine the subtle energy system of the body itself. We have both a physical structure (skeleton, organs, nervous and glandular systems etc.) and a spiritual structure called the subtle or etheric body, made up of invisible energetic pathways, such as the meridian lines used in acupuncture, the aura and the chakra system. These energies, although belonging to the individual body, align with the vibrational frequencies of the universe itself.

Aspects of the subtle body

Most esoteric belief systems describe four different aspects of the subtle body. These vibrate to different energetic frequencies but are all interrelated.

ETHERIC BODY

When people say they can "see" someone's aura, they are perceiving the etheric body around the frame of the physical one. There is also an energetic exchange between the etheric body and the physical body. In traditional Chinese medicine, this interface is the invisible system of pathways known as the meridians, carrying subtle energy, or *chi*, throughout the body. The chakras act as the doorways of energy flow from higher dimensions to lower ones. For example, energy passes directly from the chakra system of the etheric body to the physical body. The etheric and physical body rely on each other for the interplay of vibrational energy.

ASTRAL BODY

Unlike the etheric body, the astral body is not always superimposed on the physical body and is often the conduit for movement beyond the body. It is believed that alignment with the astral body occurs while altering one's state of consciousness during dreaming and astral projection. The astral body is also known as the "emotional body". Abnormal energy flow within the astral body is connected with emotional imbalance, which indirectly influences the individual's physical health, just as emotional stress eventually leads to disease.

MENTAL BODY

The mental body is of a higher frequency than the astral body. It is associated with the mind, expressions of abstract intellect and the Higher Self. No one has yet been able to measure energy on this level, although those who claim to "see" subtle energy view the mental body as being made up of the core thought forms, or ideas, of an individual's beliefs and perceptions.

CAUSAL BODY

The causal body resonates to a higher octave than the mental body. Individual emotions and ideas are no more. This is the energy plane of pure abstract ideas, of the essence of things, far beyond illusions of form or appearance. The causal body is sometimes considered to be the Higher Self resonating to Plato's Forms, with its own chakra system feeding energy to the mental body. It is not easy to form a concept of the causal body, but it is considered in Vedantic and yogic philosophy to be the vehicle, or veil, for the soul itself.

The Buddha of Infinite Illumination, depicted here in a 17th-century painting, sits atop his lotus pedestal, holding sacred flames. In Buddhism, it is thought that a person dedicates themselves to achieving the same enlightenment as the Buddha, accessing the soul or Higher Self via the energy of the subtle body.

States of consciousness

From the trance of the pilgrims who went to be healed at the Temple of Asclepius in Ancient Greece to the conditions researched by the neuroscientists of today, altered states of consciousness remain riddled with mysterious overtones. The word "trance" derives from a Latin word meaning "to cross" and "to pass over" and a trance-like state is important for anyone who wants to carry out mystical or psychic work. "Trance" can refer to an out-of-body experience, a state of hyper-suggestibility, such as hypnotism, and an altered state of awareness. The latter is usually a condition in which you transcend normal consciousness, often referred to in religious circles as "ecstasy".

Milton Erickson, the founder of hypnotherapy, introduced the hypnotic trance to orthodox medicine and currently neurologists and parapsychologists, such as Charles Tart, are exploring the trance state in both its cognitive function and its mystical capacity.

Timothy Leary

Psychologist Timothy Leary (1920–1996) proposed the "eight-circuit Model of Consciousness" in the 1970s. He believed that the human mind consisted originally of seven neurological circuits, which when activated created different levels of consciousness; he later included an eighth level. Leary thought that most people experience the first three circuits at some time in their lives, but that the last four would be triggered as human consciousness evolved. He also believed that some people can shift to higher circuits using techniques such as yoga, meditation, visualization or mind-altering drugs. These four "stellar" circuits deal with psychic and mystical states of mind. It is these altered states of consciousness, when we move out of the conscious world of self and into the stream of the universe, that our psychic perception comes into play.

The seven states of consciousness

According to various Eastern philosophies, including those of Buddhism and Hinduism, there are usually seven states of consciousness.

First state In dreamless sleep, we have no experience of self. Likened to the unconscious, there is "no one at home" or "peeping through the net curtains" to see what is outside oneself or within oneself.

Second state In dreaming sleep, there is a vague sense of the "I" and our thoughts, images and emotions stir into dreams. These occasionally arise in consciousness when we experience lucid dreaming, in which we "know" we are dreaming the dream.

Third state This is our waking state, where most of us believe we are truly awake. We know who we are. We are conscious of ourselves, but on a very personal level. We get on with life. This is the state that gives us the illusion that we're fully conscious.

Fourth state Also known as satori in Zen Buddhism, this state is about self-observation; a consciousness of the Higher Self, but a detachment from thoughts. It is an objective awareness of actions, experiences and an ability to remain detached from negative or positive emotions, no matter what is going on. It is the ability to perceive the whole of life as an interesting experience; it is to be mindful yet unaffected.

Fifth state This is samadhi, the state of stillness, the meditative state of "no mind". It is where we are still conscious but not aware of self or separateness from external objects. We are both the object and the one who sees the object. This is the state that most shamans achieve, to be able to mediate in the spirit world effectively.

Sixth state This is when we experience both the moment of being at one with the universe and its divine purpose, and a sense of our own autonomy as part of that oneness.

Seventh state Finally, in the seventh state of cosmic consciousness, we merge all sense of our individuality into the One. Often referred to as nirvana, it is where we are reunited with the Source.

Are you psychic?

At this point, you would probably like to know how psychic you really are. If you've already done the right-brain, left-brain test (see page 23), you'll know that right-brain-dominant people find it easier to develop their psychic

Your psychic potential

The following statements, describing situations that you might or might not have experienced, will give you clues as to your psychic potential. The more of these you have experienced, the more likely it is that you can develop your psychic powers.

❋ You often experience déjà vu – the feeling that you've been in that moment before, with the same actions, words, thoughts, people and/or surroundings. It is like a scene from a play taking place all over again.

❋ You think about someone and/or pick up the phone to call them, just as they think about/call you.

❋ Sometimes you say exactly the same thing as your partner at exactly the same moment.

❋ You meet someone for the first time and feel that you've known them in a previous life.

❋ Your gut instinct tells you to do one thing; your rational mind another. You trust in your sixth sense and are right.

❋ You become emotional around the time of the full moon.

❋ You have a vivid imagination.

❋ Sometimes your dreams come true.

powers. Don't worry if you discovered that you are left-brain dominant – the exercises in this book will inspire you and give you insight into developing your innate psychic gifts. If you want to do something badly enough, it will happen – that's the power of your mind. These and the following pages (36–9) will help you evaluate your psychic powers as they are now.

* You know and believe that there are guardian angels or spirits who are watching over you.

* When you're travelling and you lose your way, you can usually sense the right direction to take to find your path again.

* You keep having flashes of intuition about things that eventually do take place.

* You have had a truly enlightening or life-enhancing moment, or have felt "at one" with the universe.

How psychic are you?

Do you think you might be psychic, but are not quite sure? Look through these questions and answer, "Yes/Often", "Yes/Sometimes" or "No/Never".

Y/O	Y/S	N/N	
❑	❑	❑	Do you ever "see" things that others can't "see"?
❑	❑	❑	Are your first impressions usually "spot on"?
❑	❑	❑	Do you often know what someone else is going to say before they actually say it?
❑	❑	❑	Can you make accurate predictions?
❑	❑	❑	Do you believe you can make something happen, as if by magic?
❑	❑	❑	Do you think you can change the way somebody feels about you?
❑	❑	❑	Is your mental power more important to you than your physical strength?
❑	❑	❑	Do you feel "in tune" with certain people?
❑	❑	❑	Have you ever dreamed you were flying?
❑	❑	❑	Have you ever had an out-of-body experience?
❑	❑	❑	Do you frequently consult oracles or the Tarot cards?
❑	❑	❑	Do you believe that there is universal energy flowing through everything?

RESULTS

"Yes/Often" – score 3
"Yes/Sometimes" – score 2
"No/Never" – score 1

★ If you scored over 20, you're already on your way to a good level of psychic ability.

★ If you scored 13–19 you have average psychic awareness. It's time to work on developing your powers.

★ If you scored under 12 you may be sceptical and have to do more work than you think.

Test your psychic powers

For practical evidence of your psychic powers, try out these card divination and telepathy exercises.

CARD DIVINATION

Take a pack of playing cards. Shuffle them and lay them out in rows, face down, on a table in front of you. Now concentrate on the cards and run your fingers over them. There are two versions of this psychic test.

1 Try to think approximately where one card is (let's say the Queen of Spades). When you have decided in your psychic, right-brain mind where you "feel" the card is, begin turning the cards over to see if you are right. Don't worry if you don't succeed. But if you do, then you're certainly already on the right track.

2 The second version is to point to a card and name it. Then turn it over to see if you are right.

TELEPATHY

You will be developing your powers of telepathy in Chapter Five (see page 78–85), but for now use this simple exercise to see if you are already telepathic.

1 Sit in a comfortable position and think very hard about someone you like or love. Concentrate all your energy on that person and imagine them picking up the phone, now, to text or call you. They won't know why they are calling you, but something has entered their mind that makes them realize that they must (and that's you!).

2 Concentrate for several minutes on this image. If your friend does call you, then you're on the road to telepathic success. If not, don't worry – you'll learn how to develop all your skills in the following chapters. But like any good chef, you need to do the prep first.

chapter 2

Exploring psychic power

"It's all in the imagination" is often a response from sceptics and scientists when they are discussing the existence, or otherwise, of psychic powers. Yet it is the imagination itself, one of the most powerful areas of the mind when coupled with synchronicity and the interplay of cosmic consciousness, which is the key to unlocking your power. In this chapter you'll learn techniques to develop your imagination and mental concentration, as well as the basics of psychic protection and mental concentration and how to prepare yourself for discovering the deeper levels of psychic work.

Coincidence or synchronicity?

Do you ever wonder whether an event in your life is just a coincidence or if there is more to it? Do you ever think it might be some kind of sign? Do you feel there are powers at work that we do not fully understand? For example, you are too late to catch a plane to go to a wedding, but you meet the partner of your dreams on the next plane. You notice a no-entry sign you've never seen before and when you return home you discover that you've locked yourself out of the house. You dream a strange dream and, when you tell your friend or partner, you discover that they had the same dream. The symbolic world matters to you. Are you psychic or is this synchronicity? Or is it both?

Symbolic meaning

Coincidences and chance can be measured scientifically, but "synchronicity" is a word coined by psychologist Carl Jung for "meaningful coincidence". Still unexplainable, it is a set of occurrences that are not logically or causally related, but give us a unique, mysterious experience. We place a personal value or meaning on bringing together symbols, or events or experiences that relate to each other symbolically. We see them as part of each other and they matter to us. Are these events pure chance or is something deeper taking place?

The beliefs of Jung

Jung thought that synchronicity revealed the interconnectedness of the universe. He believed that there were two main factors involved. First, that an unconscious image would appear, either as a physical, literal experience, or as an imagined thought or outer symbol. Secondly, an objective event would coincide with this. Each event would be as bizarre as the other. This interplay

Carl Jung, the Swiss psychiatrist (1875–1961) whose work included theories about synchronicity.

Seeing a flock of birds overhead at the same moment as hearing a song on the radio about birds is an example of synchronicity.

of conscious perception, the unconscious and the cosmic consciousness is the pathway to psychic power.

A deeper order

Jung believed that there were parallels between synchronicity, relativity and quantum mechanics. He also thought that life was not a series of random events, but rather an expression of a deeper order and that a person noticing synchronicity was engaging in some kind of spiritual awakening or "tuning in" to the cosmos. Jung also believed that anything born into a moment of time, whether literally a birth or an event, captured the quality of that moment.

Synchronicity has parallels with the Chinese Tao, Greek cosmic sympathies and the Hermetic microcosm and macrocosm. The archetypal patterns involved in synchronistic experiences are the glue that holds them together. Jung realized that synchronicity was not just a relationship between the inner human world and the external one, but was also the essence of the moment. So, if a flock of birds flies overhead just as you hear the song "Blackbird" on the radio, you are personally in tune with that moment's essence. You are going to learn to do this by developing your psychic power and being "in the moment", where all knowledge is one.

The tip of the iceberg

In *The Waking Dream: Unlocking the Symbolic Language of Our Lives*, esoteric author Ray Grasse suggests that instead of being a "rare" phenomenon, as Jung suggested, synchronicity is more likely to be all-pervasive, and that the occasional dramatic coincidence is only the tip of a larger iceberg of meaning that underlies our lives. Grasse places the discussion of synchronicity in the context of what he calls the "symbolist" world view, a traditional way of perceiving the universe that regards all phenomena as being interwoven by linked analogies or "correspondences". Though omnipresent, these correspondences tend to become obvious to us only in the case of the most startling coincidences.

Living backwards

Jung was fond of a scene in Lewis Carroll's *Alice Through the Looking Glass* and used it to explain the paradox of synchronicity. This is the moment when the Queen explains to Alice how "living backwards" can be advantageous because the memory has to work "both ways". Soon, you are going to learn how to "live backwards" by developing your right-brain thinking.

The power of the mind

From a scientific viewpoint, many theories have been put forward about how the mind can literally influence matter. This is also known as "magical thinking". One such recent theory, referred to as the Butterfly Effect, is developed in the ideas of biochemist and plant physiologist, Rupert Sheldrake (see page 28). He believed that "morphic fields" surround every living thing and influence, and are influenced by, other living things. This concept has been considered by mainstream science as mere pseudo-science and is still under investigation.

A butterfly's beating wings might create minute atmospheric changes, ultimately altering the path or manifestation of a tornado, just as our thoughts have the power to change our reality.

Mind over matter?

Many psychics think that if we believe something powerfully enough, we can make it happen. This is similar to the knock-on effect in Chaos Theory and the Butterfly Effect. The latter was coined from the title of a talk entitled "Does the flap of a butterfly's wings in Brazil set off a tornado in Texas?" by meteorologist Edward Lorenz. More recently, a scientific study, carried out at the University of Colorado at Boulder in 2007, supports the concept of the power of mind over matter.

University professor Garret Moddel aimed a beam of light at a slide and asked students to try mentally to increase the amount of reflected light. They increased the reflection of the beam by .05 percent, with a similar success rate when asked to decrease the amount of reflected light.

The imagination and the cosmic mind

So what is the imagination? It is your inner vision; the ability to form mental images. Memory and day-dreaming are also manifestations of your imagination, used daily. For example, remembering how you got from A to B relies, to some extent, on imagination; you can recall how you made the journey in images.

Developing imaginative powers will sharpen awareness of your own desires. Imagine what you intend to achieve, then visualize climbing your mountain to success, create a protective psychic light around you and begin to access the sixth sense of your imagination.

With the power of your imagination and changing consciousness, you can begin to interweave with the cosmic mind. It is through this "web" that you begin to discover hidden knowledge about others, meet spirit guides or guardian angels, and learn that the future and the past can be accessed as easily as you sit there now, aware of the present.

Using your imagination

Do you think in pictures or do you have a vivid memory for numbers or words? The nature of the imagination is more mysterious than we think. You use it in creative writing, painting, playing an instrument, visualization, relaxation, meditation techniques – and psychic work. But your imagination isn't just about perceiving mental images; it encompasses all the senses. To understand this try the following:

* Sit comfortably, eyes closed. Imagine hearing your favourite song. As you listen, imagine you can smell baking bread.
* Relax and close your eyes. Imagine touching a cat. What does it feel like in your mind?
* Taste a lemon. Is it sharp and bitter in your mind?
* Now imagine feeling angry.
* Now switch your mood to feeling elated.

Changing levels of consciousness

To access your sixth sense, you need to alter your level of consciousness to that used in meditation, hypnosis and the almost trance-like state of mystics and channellers. In hypnosis, for example, we allow ourselves to drift into a different, less-awake state, yet we are still mentally alert. It seems we are more likely to permeate the barriers and blockages of our mindset in an alert state of self-observation when it is coupled with the stilled state of the trance.

Brain waves

Scientists noted that consciousness alters due to the change in brain-wave frequency. It seems that the psychic state is most accessible when the brain is vibrating at alpha or theta frequencies or fluctuating between the two. When we wander into a dream world, then feel sad at a memory before returning to rational thinking, brain waves move from alpha, theta and then to beta. Consciousness is not lost, it is simply altered. According to Hans Berger (see box below), closing the eyes causes the brain to generate alpha waves. In this mildly altered state we can begin to harness the psychic power of the mind.

Types of brain wave

Brain-wave frequency was discovered by Hans Berger in the 1920s. Named "alpha", "beta", "theta" and "delta" after the letters in the Greek alphabet, these brain waves correlate to various mental functions.

Alpha waves correspond to dream states, including hypnosis and day-dreaming.

Beta waves correspond to our wakeful, rational mind.
Theta waves correspond to our emotional, feeling, state of mind.
Delta waves represent total unconsciousness.

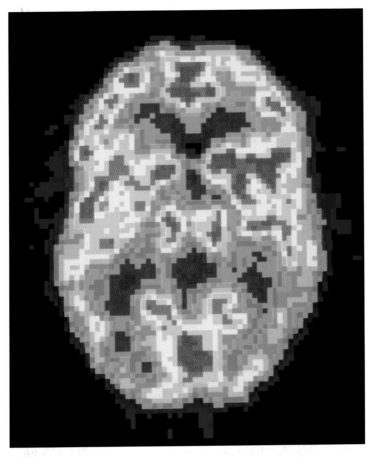

A Positron Emission Tomography (PET) scan of the human brain during REM (rapid eye movement) sleep. Colour-coding depicts active cerebral brain areas (red) through to inactive areas (blue).

Creative visualization

Visualization techniques promote positive, creative thinking and encourage the use of right brain and of theta and alpha waves. By holding specific images in your mind, you will be less likely to be invaded by rogue thoughts. Visualizing these mental images is like watching a movie or gazing at a "still" photograph.

LIMBERING UP

You can practise this exercise at any time of day. The more often you practise, the more you'll prepare yourself for the time when you visualize your success, happiness or spiritual contact. If you find you can't visualize in this way, keep trying. It will happen.

1 Sit in a quiet place and close your eyes. Think of something you like doing – for example, playing tennis, eating a meal, chatting to a friend or strumming a guitar. Now form a mental picture of it in your mind. Start with a simple short "clip". This can be "still" or a "movie", whichever is easier to "see".

2 Now try to visualize someone you love, a favourite pet, a much-loved book or an event you enjoy. Stay longer with the images; create a visual story in your mind.

BRAIN WORKOUT

This exercise forces you to use the parts of your brain that you may never have used before. Once you've got the hang of these techniques, try those on the next pages.

1 Sit in a quiet place and close your eyes. Imagine you are writing a high random number, such as 2,568, using your non-writing hand on a blackboard.

2 Imagine encircling the number in chalk with your writing hand. Now rub out the number with your non-writing hand and the circle with your writing hand.

3 Then write the next number in the sequence (counting down): 2,567. Now imagine rubbing out the number with your non-writing hand and rubbing out the circle with your writing hand.

4 Repeat this method with the next number in the sequence: 2,566 and so on, until you find it easy to visualize this exercise.

Visualizing colours

Visualization is key to achieving astute psychic power. Imagining colour is one of the simplest visualization techniques, helping you to open the pathway to sensing the universe in a psychic way. Concentrate on one colour at a time and discover how, for example, red is not just about "seeing" red, but "experiencing" it, too.

Each colour has archetypal qualities: blue helps us relax, but it also represents water, nurturing, spiritual openness and female receptivity. Red is dynamic and passionate (see opposite), representing courage, male energy and competitiveness. These two exercises help you "imagine" two primary colours and feel their effect. You need 10 minutes per exercise.

SEEING BLUE

1 Sit somewhere quiet and make sure you are not going to be interrupted. Close your eyes and create a mental picture of being connected to the earth, as if your feet have roots reaching down through its crust. Now imagine that deep within the ground the colour blue permeates the earth's interior. Realize that blue is the colour of calm and serenity.

2 Next imagine that the colour blue begins to slowly work its way up through your feet and then your legs, your torso, your arms and your head. Take it slowly.

See the colour filling you, permeating every cell in your body, until you are completely blue. Now you will feel totally calm and relaxed.

3 Gradually let the blue colour wash away, back down into the earth, before you leave the technique. If you can, create a feeling of calm by visualizing blue. Open your eyes; return to normality.

SEEING RED

1 Close your eyes. Create a mental picture of a huge bubble, filled with the colour red, above your head.

2 Reach up and pierce the bubble with one finger, without bursting it. Imagine the colour red slowly flowing through your fingers into your hand and through your body, until you are filled with red.

3 Now imagine you feel full of desire: hot, invincible, fiery, infallible. Let the red wash back up through your body to your fingertips, back into the bubble.

4 Imagine seeing something you want in the bubble. You can get what you want simply by connecting to the bubble of desire. Let it flow into you as you let the colour red flow through you.

More colour work

Try another simple visualization technique. You can repeat this exercise as often as you like, to develop your personal skills. This technique is also useful for cleansing and vitalizing your subtle body energies before doing any psychic work. It puts you into a peaceful, yet aware, state of mind. Sit somewhere quiet and make sure you are not going to be interrupted.

1 Close your eyes and imagine a rainbow surrounding and encircling you. Open your hands as if to embrace the rainbow and let the first colour, red, fill your hands, the colour passing into you, through you and all around you.

2 Now do the same with the other six colours: orange, then yellow, green, blue, indigo, violet – until all the colours have flowed through you. Try to experience the principal quality associated with each colour as it passes through you. Red is associated with passion; orange with inspiration; yellow with playfulness; green with desire; blue with serenity; indigo with spiritual understanding and violet with universal completeness. Open your eyes; return to normality.

Psychic preparation

Before setting off on any new adventure, you need to prepare your mind, body and spiritual self. It's not a good idea to rush ahead to Chapter Three (pages 86–133) to do aura-reading or faith-healing if you have not laid the essential groundwork first. It's like gradually building up certain muscles to train for a new sport. Psychologically you need to be strong in yourself, confident in your power and ability and also aware that if you are truly looking for positive feedback from the universe, then that is what you will encounter. If you are negative, you're more likely to meet negative energy.

With a little work on yourself and some practice, a willingness to deepen your psychic journey, not forgetting all-important protective techniques, you'll be armed with the right purpose, belief and spiritual strength to develop your powers.

Making friends with yourself is essential to developing personal psychic power. If you're not aware of your virtues and faults, if you can't accept who you are, then you're unlikely to be able to integrate your psychic ability with the spiritual world and the interconnected universe. It's not just about being friends with the outer "you"; you must also be able to like the inner "you". Now is the time to prepare yourself for positive psychic work and make sure that you are truly grounded and stabilized in "reality".

Strengthening the psyche

With a mixture of concentration, grounding and self-confidence you will be ready to work with your psychic powers. Concentration is especially important, to enable you to visualize, meditate on and stick to your psychic goals. This energy lets your mind focus on one object, idea, project or thought without being led astray by the ramblings of your mental orchestra.

Watching time

Think about how many things go through your mind every minute; think about how many feelings, thoughts, sounds, tastes, smells, ideas and images you have to process and how, if you can clear your head of all those babblings, you will have a clear view of where you are going. This exercise will help you start this process.

Many of us lack concentration. We drift off into a dreamy world of endless thoughts; some positive, some negative. We also have a problem with time. We either panic about it or get bored with it. The art of concentrating enables you to detach from such chattering thoughts inside your head. This exercise also opens you to the real meaning of time and how it is only as long or as short as you imagine it to be.

Find a quiet place to sit and place a watch with a second hand in front of you. Now clock-watch for at least three minutes. Sit and just watch the second hand moving around the clock face. If you find your attention wandering, then start again for another three minutes, counting either in your head or out loud with each second, until you get to 180 seconds. It will seem longer than you had imagined it would!

Getting grounded

"Grounding" literally means being in touch with the "real" world. If you can keep track of your own normal mindset, you'll find that it is far easier to engage with cosmic consciousness. Being grounded is essential when you "come back" from a meditative or higher consciousness state and it is vital as a platform from which to start any meditative exercise.

Do this exercise before every psychic session while you're still a beginner, as part of your ritual build-up. Once you can get to your "psychic sanctuary" as easy as blinking an eye (see pages 100–1) you can omit this exercise. But it may be important to return to it sometimes to remind yourself of your physical connection to the earth.

1 Find somewhere quiet, where you won't be interrupted. Sit cross-legged on the floor. If you find this difficult just sit in your favourite chair with your hands resting in your lap.

2 Imagine you are a beautiful oak tree in a forest glade. Imagine your branches filled with leaves and the spirits of nature, who are your guardians. You can feel the strength of your trunk, thousands of years old, and the roots reaching down into the ground beneath you.

3 Imagine you have roots growing out of your feet or from your pelvic floor grounding you in the depths of the earth and nourishing your whole being from that source.

4 Once you have imagined this for a few minutes, you can take a deep breath and relax. Open your eyes and know that this exercise will always ground you.

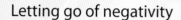

Letting go of negativity

Self-confidence and believing in your psychic power is half the battle in becoming psychic. If you truly have faith in yourself, as well as belief in your psychic abilities, then you will discover that you can accomplish much in your own self-development and heal others, too. This exercise is about thinking in a certain way. If you can think yourself positive, then you will be positive. If any negative thoughts arise, say, "No, I will not have negative thoughts. They are banished from my mind."

If you have low self-esteem try to do this exercise every day for a week. If you have serious confidence issues, this exercise may not work the first time you try it, but it is an effective way to stop that babbling brook of negativity taking hold of you – so keep practising. You will need a piece of paper and pencil and a bowl of pebbles.

1 First look at yourself in a mirror. Do you like what you see? If not, articulate what you don't like, also your fears, your worries and your woes. Don't be tempted to deceive yourself by leaving anything out. Now write down a list of all these things.

2 Count out some pebbles. These represent the negative things you have just written down.

3 Sit somewhere quiet and place the pebbles in a bowl.

4 Remove the pebbles one by one, placing them on your written list. As you position each one say, "I have belief in myself; I am confident of my success and my psychic ability."

5 Once you have emptied the bowl, you have emptied your mind of all negativity. Now discard the pebbles. You have thrown away all your vulnerability.

Detachment or mindfulness

Objectivity is one of the other necessary qualities for psychic work, especially when you are dealing with other people whose emotions, feelings, auras and body energies may be negative, distorted or invasive. Being uninvolved doesn't mean you don't care; it just means you won't allow your inner energy to be put out of balance by others.

A calm, relaxed state is just as important as a strong psyche. Meditation is a key to good relaxation. Meditate once a day to still your mind and, as a beginner, before you do any psychic work. Read the section on meditation techniques in Chapter Three (see pages 106–9).

Negative thoughts are like a bowl of pebbles; they can rest heavily on your mind, but they can also be discarded whenever you like.

A psychics' code of conduct

Fear of "what may be" and the popularized scepticism present in the scientific world can be a hindrance to psychic development. But armed with self-belief, a little curiosity and keeping the well-being of all concerned in mind (plus learning some psychic self defence basics), there is little to harm you. Establish the following major points from the start.

* You are only doing this work for the good of others and of yourself.

* You can control your thoughts – your thoughts don't control you.

* You truly believe in your powers.

* You are responsible for your own choices.

* The laws of attraction work both ways – if you are negative you will attract negative energy to you. If you are positive you will receive positive energy.

* You are always objective and must never get emotionally involved with those you are trying to help.

Now you must create what is considered to be a universal psychic protection field (see opposite), to protect your aura, body energy and psychic senses. Do this before you do carry out any serious psychic work.

How to create a psychic protection field

This exercise has become a classic among psychic practitioners – it is one of the most straightforward visualization techniques available to us. It enables you to approach difficult or unfamiliar situations without worry of psychic overload or attack, either from other people or from negative energy fields.

1 Sit in a quiet place and with your eyes closed, passive yet alert, mindful yet relaxed, imagine a bright light in front of you and focus your mind on it. Gradually imagine the light enveloping you, surrounding your whole body like a bubble that is all around you and beneath you, too.

2 Visualize the outer surface of the bubble hardening, like a protective crystal encasing you; the light inside washing over and through you and your aura.

3 Now say to yourself, "This light will protect me from all negative energies. This field of light will be with me always. No negative thoughts will ever be entertained by me."

4 Hold the image for a couple of minutes and then take a deep breath and let go of it gradually. Before leaving your imagined bubble of protection, say, "My bubble is always there, even though I cannot visualize it." Now open your eyes.

ESP, sixth sense and intuition

Extra-sensory perception (ESP) is the more scientific definition for "intuition", "the sixth sense" and, more popularly, a "hunch", "feeling", "gut instinct" or a feeling of being "spooked". Most psychic skills, such as precognition, clairvoyance, telepathy, channelling and mediumship involve some kind of ESP – a phenomenon that is yet to be explained scientifically.

The phrase "the sixth sense", as a form of intuition, was coined by Charles Richet, the Nobel Prize-winning French physiologist, in his *Notre Sixième Sens* (1926). He concluded that there must be a sixth sense sensitive to specific vibrations that none of the other senses could process.

The word "intuition" comes from a Latin root meaning "to look at" or "watch over". Most people recognize intuition to be a sudden awareness or complete "knowing". Sometimes it happens so quickly that you miss what it is you know. It is as if you know that if you do X, then Y will be the result, but you don't know how you know.

Instant connection

How intuition, or sixth sense, actually manifests is open to controversy. If the left brain equates with intellectual knowledge and the right brain with concepts, imagination and feelings, psychologists have concluded that intuition is a process of right-brain functioning, fuelled by an emotional trigger. An emotion that feels good implies that you're going in the right direction; a negative emotion that you're off course. A more spiritual approach is that the sixth sense is an instant connection to our unconscious as we tap into the universal storehouse of knowledge. Alice Bailey, an early 20th-century esoteric writer, believed that intuition was a divine power working through us. However it manifests, intuition "watches over" us, too.

Charles Richet, the physiologist, who coined the phrase "the sixth sense".

Developing your sixth sense

We use our five senses without much conscious awareness. Before working with your sixth sense, you first need to tone up your other five senses so that they can work in tandem with your sixth. Many psychics, such as clairvoyants or channellers, often experience the spiritual world via sight, sound, touch and hearing – these sense become conduits for their sixth sense.

LISTENING TO SILENCE

1 Try to listen to the sounds coming out of apparent silence. Sit somewhere where you believe there is no noise, such as in a library, a country lane, the top of a mountain or in a room that no one else can enter.

2 Sit quietly and listen. You will still hear sounds, however silent you think the environment is. Sound is relative. If you are in the world, you will hear something.

SMELLING A ROSE

1 The fragrances of the universe are profoundly awakening. Take a rose or some other perfumed flower. Close your eyes. Just let the smell enter your nostrils.

2 As you breathe in the fragrance think laterally. Instead of just thinking, "This is a rose and it has this smell because it is a rose", ask yourself why a rose smells like a rose? Are there are other smells coming from the rose that you hadn't noticed before? Perhaps its stem has a different fragrance or the sun's warmth on a single petal may subtly alter its scent from that of the others. What about the garden where you picked the rose? Can you smell it, or the wider countryside, or the world itself? Can you smell the universe in a rose?

THE POWER OF TOUCH

1 Place a leaf, piece of fruit or a crystal in the palm of your hand. All these objects have their own natural energy fields.

2 Sit quietly, close your eyes and concentrate on the object and what it feels like in your palm.

3 Now touch the object with your other hand. Then move that hand 2–3in (5–7cm) away and feel the subtle energy exuding from the object. Experiment with other people's possessions – this exercise will also help you develop your powers of psychometry, which is divination using someone's belongings (see pages 184–7).

PERIPHERAL VISION

Much of what we see passes us by. We see what we want to see. This exercise will make you more aware of things you wouldn't normally see, preparing you to start to see auras and other energy fields, whether spiritual or material.

1 Hold your finger out in front of you at arm's length and eye level and stare at it. As you focus, be aware of everything else around it, but without focusing on anything else.

2 Begin to note other things in the room or landscape. Gradually increase your peripheral awareness as you look out from the corners of your eyes, but still look straight ahead. Be aware of things going on almost behind you.

Working with the sixth sense

This exercise will help you to develop your right-brain intuitive and sixth-sense processes. The more you come to trust your intuition and the more you practise visualization techniques, the easier it will be to carry out psychic work.

1 Make a conscious decision to be on your own. Choose a suitable place in which you can ensure a deep level of receptivity. Relax and breathe quietly.

2 Close your eyes and imagine that you are walking down a long road. To the right of you are fields in a beautiful landscape. To the left are high cliffs and a cave, where you decide to stop for a while.

3 In the cave is a golden mat. As you sit down on it to rest, a shimmering shaft of pure white light beams down on you through a crevice above you. You feel the power of this spiritual energy filling your body, flowing through every pore and into every cell, from your head right down to your toes.

4 Now, with your energy levels topped up, you walk out of the cave and on down the road. You approach a corner. What is around the corner? Intuitively you know. At this moment, imagine whatever comes into your being around the corner. For example, imagine you are about to encounter a man on a bike or a woman in a red dress, a dog, a friendly rhino – whatever comes into your mind.

5 Now turn the corner in your imagination and actually meet the entity you had intuited. Say "hello", offer your best wishes and then continue to go on your way.

6 Come out of your visualization gradually and relax back to normal. Now, for the rest of the day and for several days afterwards, every time you turn a corner and walk down a different street, walk into a shop or walk out of the house, let your right brain take over from your left-brain's thoughts and push yourself to pursue your intuition. Follow up your hunches and work with your sixth sense until it becomes an everyday experience. You may not always be right, but with practice the sixth sense can become your most effective sense.

Precognition, premonition, déjà vu

The idea that we can see into the future has confounded both the scientist and the mystic alike. No one has yet proved or disproved that this is a genuine psychic power, and the mystery continues to provide much food for thought in both scientific and esoteric circles.

Precognition

"Precognition" is derived from a Latin word meaning "foreknowledge" and is the experience of direct knowledge of the future, occurring mostly in dreams but also in visions or thoughts. It can also be induced through divinational trances and altered states of consciousness.

British aeronautical engineer J.W. Dunne discovered that precognitive dreams are more common than we realize. His first such dream occurred in 1898, when he dreamed of the correct time before actually waking up. With over 20 personal precognitive experiences, he developed his theory of consciousness and time. Dunne researched both precognitive dreams and the hypnagogic state – where we hover between sleep and wakefulness. He believed that our experience of time as a linear phenomenon is an illusion and argued that past, present and future are simultaneous, only experienced sequentially because of our cognitive perception. In the dreaming and hypnagogic state, our mind is free from the constraints of mental processing and able to perceive past and future events with equal facility.

Another theory put forward by parapsychologists is that psychokinetic energy is unleashed when the individual experiences precognition, setting off a chain reaction in the universe, so that the foreseen event happens. Contemporary parapsychologists believe that what happens through psychokinetic energy in the future may also influence the past.

How often have you dreamed or imagined an event, only for it to come true? Did it happen because you thought it or have you bypassed the linear perception of time and seen into the future because past, present and future are all just the "eternal now"? To develop your own precognitive powers meditate on these words: "The present is the past of the future and the present is the future of the past. The present is both future and past."

Reflected in the present is our past; can our future be seen in the present moment, too?

Gazing into a crystal ball can reveal patterns and signs that are symbolic of the present moment or of our future, just like the images we see in our dreams.

Premonition

Often confused with precognition, "premonition" is derived from the Latin word meaning a "forewarning". Premonitions are emotional reactions or feelings that something is going to happen, but the individual doesn't know what – they can't put a name to it. This can often occur in dreams, but it's more usual when we are wide awake and have a sense of some future event that is usually not welcome. We have fearful expectations for others and ourselves and often we "know" that things are not going to go well. For example, perhaps going to an interview suddenly brings on apprehension about meeting the interviewer and a fear that we won't get the job. Psychologists suggest that this is because we are more sensitive to things that make us feel anxious rather than those that make us happy, but this doesn't explain why we actually experience this "forewarning".

Déjà vu

Déjà vu has often been referred to as "remembering the future". A strangely paradoxical effect, the French words *déjà vu* actually mean "already seen". The phrase was coined by Émile Boirac in his book of psychic research *L'Avenir des Sciences Psychiques*.

When you experience déjà vu, you have a feeling that you are repeating something that has already happened – perhaps in another dimension or time. Another experience is recognizing something about that moment; almost as if you are witnessing yourself doing something a split second before you do it. It feels both familiar yet strange.

The vision hypothesis

Many scientists and psychologists have tried to prove déjà vu to be merely a neurological fault between short-term and long-term memory, while parapsychologists believe it is related to past-life experiences. Another hypothesis being explored is that of vision. The theory suggests that one eye may record what is seen fractionally faster than the other, creating the recollected sensation when the "same" scene is viewed milliseconds later by the opposite eye.

Other forms of déjà vu

Other forms of déjà vu include *déjà vécu* – already lived; *déjà senti* – already felt; *déjà visité* – already visited; and *jamais vu*, where a person momentarily does not recognize a word, person or place that they already know. The phenomenon known as *presque vu*, almost seen, is the sensation of being on the brink of a discovery or a revelation. Often very distracting, *presque vu* rarely leads to an actual breakthrough and is usually described as having something "on the tip of my tongue".

Clairvoyance

"Clairvoyance" is from the French word *clairvoyant,* meaning "seeing clearly". This phenomenon is often interpreted as having "second sight" or being able to see with the Third Eye or the "inner eye". This is the ability to be acutely aware of other people, "seeing" them through a perception that is not beyond the five known senses. Clairvoyants can retrieve hidden information about other people, experiences and events, find missing objects and often see a person's aura.

"Clear awarenesses" are reported in ancient Hindu texts and referred to as *siddhis* – a kind of perfect awareness achieved through meditation. In the world of mediumship, the words "clairvoyant" and "clairaudience" usually refer to seeing or feeling the presence of spirits, rather than the psychic perception that links them with objects or people.

How to develop your clairvoyant skills

First, how clairvoyant do you think you are? Read these statements but don't think too long about them before agreeing or disagreeing. If you answer "yes" to at least three of these statements, then you are probably a natural clairvoyant.

Y   N

❑   ❑   I often "see" what people are doing when they are somewhere else and not in view.

❑   ❑   I sense immediately if someone is kind or unkind.

❑   ❑   If a friend has a problem and needs help, I know before they tell me.

❑   ❑   I can read other people's minds.

❑   ❑   I have visions of the future that come true

Other associated techniques

"Clairaudience" comes from the French words *clair* and *audience* meaning "clear" and "hearing". Clairaudience is simply "clear listening" but via ESP. You are using your normal "hearing" sense, but you also pick up sounds, music, rhythms and vibrational tones that are not always apparent to the ordinary ear. Many clairaudients can hear voices of the living who are not present as well as spirit voices. It is believed that those who have practised meditation and have reached a higher level of consciousness can activate their "third ear" and hear the music of the celestial spheres.

"Clairsentience" comes from the French *clair*, "clear", and sentience. This method is used by psychics to pick up the vibrational energy of other people, as well as moods, emotions and feelings. "Claircognizance" is picking up psychic knowledge about other people.

We all have flashes of intuition, or moments when we can "see" the answer we've been looking for. Unlocking your psychic power depends on using all your senses as well as developing your sixth.

Simple oracle reading

Many people use a book, such as the Bible, a dictionary or even the complete works of Shakespeare, as an oracle for divining the future. This simple, but fun, way to consult an oracle can be tried daily to tone up your intuitive powers of interpretation.

You can also use your mind as if it were an oracle, to divine how the day ahead will be. Simply close your eyes, empty all thoughts from your mind and then say, "Give me a clue as to how today will be." The first thought that comes to you, whatever it is, will have important insight and relevance to the day ahead.

1 Find a favourite book, go to a quiet place and relax. With the book in front of you, riffle through the pages, back and forth, with your eyes closed. As you do so think of a simple question, such as, "Who will be important for me today?" or "Will I get held up going to work?" Or simply think of the day ahead and what you would most like to happen.

2 Now stop at a page that "feels" right to you. Then, without looking, touch it with your finger. Open your eyes and read the words nearest, and beneath, your finger. They may make up a sentence or a phrase that seems to have meaning for you, or simply be one or two words that you can remember easily.

3 Throughout the day, keep a note of how the words in the book had relevance to your question, with particular reference to the people you bumped into and events that you did not expect. You will find some amazing correspondences.

Wish for the day

Try out this exercise either last thing at night or first thing in the morning. It is part of learning to access your psychic powers. Make sure you are relaxed, calm and centred before you start.

1 Close your eyes and imagine you are on a wide sandy beach. If you are lucky enough to live beside a beach then you can do this there, early in the morning.

2 As you walk along the beach you find a large stick and write a message to the universe giving thanks for all you have and for what you wish will happen today.

3 Imagine you are writing, "I am the designer of my destiny", then write your wish for the day in the sand. Don't write something unrealistic such as, "I wish I could win the lottery." Ask for something simple, like a really nice day and for everyone you love to have a nice day, too. Then imagine the tide coming in and washing away your words. The sea of cosmic consciousness has taken your words, to connect you to the harmonious workings of the universe.

4 Come out of your visualization and thank the universe for letting you make a wish and for allowing you to write down what you wanted for the day ahead.

5 During the day observe whether the thing you wished for happens. (If it doesn't then you may not have had total faith in yourself and the power of universal attraction. Try again.)

Using hunches and synchronicity

This exercise will push your intuitive side to work in everyday circumstances and is a good focus when you start to keep a journal of your experiences in psychic development. The more you observe and record experiences such as hunches or apparent coincidences, the more you are developing your psychic powers at the same time.

The Empress

During the day, perhaps just on your way to and from work, there will be moments when you have a "hunch"; at other moments you might experience synchronicity. A hunch might be when you are sitting on the train and have a feeling that the person in front of you will get off at the next stop – and he does. A moment of synchronicity is when a woman walks past in a red coat at the moment you were thinking about buying red apples.

For Carl Jung, synchronicity provided evidence for his theories of archetypes and the collective unconscious. The Empress Tarot card represents the Earth Mother archetype, a concept found in many different cultures around the world.

1 On the first day, just note any hunches or moments of synchronicity that you become aware of.

2 The next day, act on any hunches. For example, if you have a hunch that turning right down a street rather than left down another is going to make your drive to work more pleasant, follow that intuition. Also note any intuitive moments you ignored. By choosing to use your rational mind, you actually made a wrong choice.

3 Notice any synchronicity. For example, what is the meaning behind seeing a car go by bearing a number plate with your birthday on it? Could it be a reminder that you need to attend to your own needs, or that perhaps the number will be of significance to you again at some point?

4 If you have a choice to make, for example to call up someone about a new job, or not to do so as you feel it's safer to stay where you are, ask your intuitive self (your Higher Self, your Third Eye, your link with the cosmos) what is your true soul's intention? Is it to move on and take a risk, or to stick with the tried and trusted? The soul will always answer truthfully. If you still aren't sure, continue to the next step.

5 Toss a coin. Promise yourself that if it falls heads you *will* change your career, if it falls tails you *won't*. Say it falls heads, but deep down your soul is crying out to you to stay where you are, you will feel this. Say it falls tails and yet your soul is desperate for you to move on, you will know this. Deep within you, your soul knows what you really want, so whichever way the coin falls, you will know the truth from your clairvoyant awareness. The only true answer lies within. Trust in the soul within, not in the flip of the coin without.

Telepathy

From the Greek words *tele* meaning "distant" and *patheia* "to be affected by", telepathy is the transference of thoughts, feelings or ideas between two or more individuals via the psychic sense. Classical scholar Frederick W.H. Myers, the founder of the Society for Psychical Research, coined this word in 1882 as a replacement for the original term "thought-transference".

A common example of tuning in to our psychic mind is when we know someone is about to call us, before they actually do.

Parapsychologists refer to any form of psychic phenomenon as "psi", which is the 23rd letter of the Greek alphabet and the first letter of "psyche" in Greek. It is used as a generic word to cover all psychic phenomena, experiences or events that cannot be explained by established physical principles.

Types of telepathy

Parapsychologists divide telepathy into three specific types.

* "Intuitive" telepathy is the transfer of information about the past, future or present state of an individual's mind, through psi, to another individual.
* Emotive telepathy, also known as "emotional transfer", is the process of transferring sensations and feelings through altered states of consciousness.
* "Superconscious telepathy" involves tapping into the cosmic consciousness to access the collective pool of wisdom.

There is also a kind of spontaneous telepathy that occurs without making any conscious effort. This is when, for example, your partner's car breaks down

Psychokinesis

If we can psychically affect and influence the thoughts of other people, it is believed that we also have the power to move and influence inanimate objects. This is known as "psychokinesis".

From the Greek *psyche* meaning "soul" or "animating spirit" and *kinesis* meaning "motion", this term was coined by researcher and writer Henry Holt in 1914 to describe how the mind, or "soul", has the power to move objects without physical influence. Self-levitation, shape-shifting, teleportation, thought-form projection and object deformation all come under the umbrella term "psychokinesis". The term is still used in popular culture, though it originally implied the movement of objects by supernatural forces, such as ghosts and spirits, rather than by the power of the human mind.

As psychokinesis is concerned with the power of the mind over matter, much research has been carried out to prove that the mind can move objects or that it is impossible according to the laws of physics. Try for yourself. Focus, concentrate and imagine that you can shift the spoon on the table. Perhaps if you can imagine doing something, then the likelihood of really being able to do it becomes greater.

and they send out signals of anger and frustration to you at home. Even before they reach for the phone, you pick up on these signals telepathically and phone them first.

Telepathy is fun to try out, but you need a friend or partner who truly believes they can send or receive messages, too. It's no good asking someone who doesn't believe – it simply won't work.

Uri Geller is famous for his psychokinesis, dowsing and telepathy and he has demonstrated his techniques, particularly spoon-bending, widely on television.

Transmitting colour via telepathy

Try out this telepathic exercise with a friend. First decide who will send the information and who will receive it. Make sure your friend is sitting facing away from you so that you can't cheat.

1 Centre yourselves, relax and still your minds into a meditational trance. Try not to think of anything at all.

2 The sender then thinks of a colour (this colour and no other – with no other thought). This is where your powers of concentration come to the fore. The sender mentally focuses on transmitting this colour to the receiver and writes its name on a piece of paper.

3 The receiver writes down the colour they receive. When the receiver has received the colour, they can just say, "Ready" and then the sender chooses another colour. Do this for perhaps five minutes maximum to begin with and then compare your list of colours.

4 Then complete the same exercise with the roles of sender and receiver reversed. You may find that there are not as many "hits" as you'd like, but the more you practise, the better you will become. Then you can progress to starting to use cards and other images, as described in the following pages.

Practice is the key to success in telepathy, so don't give up if you don't manage to transmit and receive messages at first. Keep trying.

Zener cards

These cards were designed by psychologist Karl Zener in the early 1930s to carry out experiments into extrasensory perception (ESP) with his colleague, J.B. Rhine. Zener cards use five very different symbols (see below). You can use this test yourself either to "predict" the cards you are about to draw from the pack and test your own clairvoyant powers, or as a useful way to help develop your telepathic powers.

In the Ganzfield Effect (see page 21), the sender is located far away from the receiver and the latter is in a controlled environment, deprived of any sensory input. You don't have to send your partner into a dark room all alone to do this, but it does help if you are in separate places, or at the very least positioned back to back.

Zener alternatives

You can either make your own Zener cards or use a deck of playing cards, Tarot cards or some other cards. They must display symbolic images, such as numbers from one to nine, a selection of runes or perhaps the names of crystals – whatever you feel most comfortable with. You can also carry out the experiment over the phone at a prearranged time.

All in the cards

This first Zener exercise (adapted to improve telepathic powers – see page 18) is fun to do, and it will also make your right-brain mind work a little harder. Try it at different times of day, such as just after waking or before going to bed, to see if there is a difference in results.

In a Zener card test, you have a one-in-five chance of picking the right card – any higher ratio of success indicates telepathic ability. It seems that the more trials you conduct in one go, the better the chances of success.

1 Sender and receiver sit back to back, or at least unable to see what the other is doing. Both relax, with pen and paper ready. Agree who is to be the sender and who is to be the receiver.

2 The sender shuffles the deck of cards, places them face down on the table, randomly drawing one card and turning it over. They concentrate on the card, thinking only of that card's image and no other, and with their right-brain mind they send the image to the receiver, saying aloud the words, "It is being sent."

3 The receiver opens their right-brain mind, to allow the image to come to them, and then draws the image on a piece of paper. When they are sure they have received the image they say, "It is received."

4 The sender can then shuffle the cards again and take another card at random. Roles should be reversed after about five tests.

Image transmission

This exercise requires a lot more concentration and psychic awareness, but once you've got used to doing the colour and card exercises (see pages 80–1 and 83), try it out.

1 With a friend, arrange a time to suit both of you, when you can be available on the phone.

2 Make the phone call and agree who will be sender and receiver for exactly five minutes, and then agree to call back for the results. Synchronize your watches and end the phone call.

3 If you are the sender, draw a picture of whatever comes into your mind, spontaneously, at that moment. As you draw (as simply as you like) keep thinking about this image all the time. Imagine it being transported by the cosmic energy field that flows through everything to your friend's mind.

4 As the receiver, open your mind to the flow of energy and when you sense an image spontaneously coming to your mind, start to draw it.

5 After the allotted time, phone each other and see what you have both drawn. The drawings may not be identical, but there may be similarities to suggest that you made some kind of telepathic contact. For example, perhaps you drew a square house with four windows and a door while your friend drew a square with a four-line cross in the middle.

Test your telepathic powers by drawing a picture and trying to send your visualization to a friend.

chapter 3

Psychic protection and healing

An essential part of psychic work is to learn how to protect yourself from negative energy. This can either come from those who project bad thoughts onto you or consciously or unconsciously try to manipulate you, or because you are more exposed to universal psychic energies when entering a psychic state of consciousness. Negative energy also creates static pools in certain houses and public places, such as dead-end streets and public places. Armed with self-protective knowledge you can ward off these energies and create your own psychic sanctuary, where you feel secure in your psychic development. The more you enhance your innate psychic healing abilities, the more positive healing energy you put out into the world and, in turn, the more the world will heal you and direct your spiritual and personal growth.

Psychic protection

Have you ever entered a room and found yourself wondering about the bad atmosphere? As humans we are all sensitive beings, capable of picking up the good and the bad atmospheres around us and so sometimes we fall prey to the negative emotions of others. Often we can get rid of this negative residue without too much difficulty, by involving ourselves in day-to-day activities or in the good company of friends and family. But at other times we need help.

Entering a new environment and feeling over-sensitive can cause us to notice negativity in many different social situations.

Psychic protection offers us a whole range of invaluable techniques we can use to keep ourselves safe. Think of it as being rather like putting on a raincoat to protect yourself from bad weather. It is important that you find a form of psychic protection that suits you and one that you can summon whenever you feel you need it.

Personal warning system

There are times when you may feel that you are under psychic threat from a specific individual. Perhaps it seems that someone is intent on making you feel uncomfortable or even fearful. Learn to isolate these feelings and work on them, using your psychic protection techniques. It could be that something unwelcome has come into contact with your aura, or that you're sensing difficult emotions from someone or from within yourself. On pages 89–93 there are some useful techniques to help you.

Simple psychic protection techniques

This is a short introduction to some of the most common methods for psychic self-protection. In many day-to-day situations we instinctively turn to these techniques to help us out.

PRAYER

To invoke a higher power to bring psychic protection:
Become calm and centred, then focus on your concept of the Divine.

BREATHING

To keep calm and become centred when you are threatened:
Focus on breathing in and out, slowly and deliberately.

BLESSING

To attract positive experiences into your life:
Give thanks to the universe for everything that is good.

AFFIRMATION

To manifest positivity in your situation and life in general:
Transmit a positive saying to your subconscious mind.

PSYCHIC WARNING

To protect yourself from psychic attack by another person:
Develop the habit of being calm and balanced.

Psychic defence

Try one of the techniques on these two pages before you go to an interview, deal with difficult people, face an exam or test of character, or have dealings with negative family members. Whatever happens, every day imagine a protective bubble of light encircling you (see page 61).

GROUNDING YOURSELF

To keep in touch with reality, repeat this technique every day before embarking on any psychic work.

1 Sit with your eyes closed and relax. Imagine you are rooted to the spot. A series of strong tree roots is growing down from your spine, penetrating the earth.

2 Now stand up, close your eyes and imagine the roots are connecting your feet to the ground and the earth. You can imagine this even when you are walking along, as each step you take brings you back in touch with your roots.

RAINBOW PYRAMID

This is a visualization that will protect your subtle body energies and aura from any outside intrusions. You can use the pyramid to envelop your car, house and loved ones, to defend them against negative energy.

1 Close your eyes and visualize that you are encased in a pyramid made up of the colours of the rainbow. Imagine that the base of the pyramid is beneath your feet and the apex above your head.

2 With your mind, "paint" the base of the pyramid beneath you in all the colours of the spectrum. Then swoosh your brush up to paint the pyramid's four sides.

3 Whenever you feel threatened or you enter a negative place, imagine that your pyramid is around you, your aura, your subtle body energy and even your protective bubble of light. This creates a double protective shield for psychic work.

IT'S ALL IN THE EYES

When you know you are about to meet someone who may have a negative influence on you, or if you've just encountered someone you intuitively know to be negative, try out these tips to counter their bad energy.

* Don't look directly into the person's eyes. Instead of making eye contact, look at the middle of their forehead, between the eyes. They won't notice the subtle variation of your gaze. When you concentrate on their Third Eye chakra they have no power over you.

* Look beyond the person, without them realizing it. In a way, you are making them invisible.

PRACTISING GAZING

If you need to practise gazing techniques further, try out these two ideas to hone your skills.

* Hold up your finger at arm's length, level with your eyes. Focus on it for a few seconds, then remove it and keep focusing on the empty spot – the air itself. Soon your eyes will refocus into the distance. Learn to hold this gaze for as long as possible.

* Hold up your finger, as before, but this time don't move it away. Look at an object in the distance, way beyond your finger – perhaps at a tree, a wall or at another building. Your finger will go out of focus. You can also try this technique out on a person. You are now looking beyond, and through, them.

Talismans

Crossing yourself is a Christian religious device that affirms faith in God. The cross is also an ancient pre-Christian symbol of faith, as is the pentagram. Used by Chinese Feng Shui masters to represent the five elements, the pentagram is a symbol that has been used by occultists, Pythagoreans and magicians, representing the microcosm and the macrocosm. When the five-pointed star is encircled, it creates a pentacle. This magic talisman is a symbol of you and the world reflected in one another. Wearing the pentagram as jewelry or drawing the shape of it in the air around you will bring instant psychic protection for your aura and subtle body energies.

Combating your own negative energy

We all have bad thoughts as well as good ones – it's only human nature. But as the ancients and Eastern philosophers knew, what you put out into the world usually comes back to you tenfold.

If you are using the power of your mind for the good of the whole and taking responsibility for that, then you must also learn to counter-balance any negative energy you might put out. We all do this by mistake, but often on purpose! We wish our boss could be eaten alive by a monster or we send out "poisonous" vibes to a business competitor. First, you should try to cultivate tolerance and acceptance of other people's faults. Next comes self-discipline. Then, lastly,

an exercise to restore the balance of energies. For example, say you talked unkindly about a colleague behind her back but you now realize that what you said was cruel or just downright unnecessary. Close your eyes, enter a quiet trance-like state and start to put out affirmations to your colleague, plus blessings, goodness and even regrets. Perhaps repeat a favourite prayer or poem to her. Ask forgiveness from the cosmos and then say, "And let the light of the universe shine through her every day."

Pentacle defence

In addition to wearing specific crystals or runes or repeating spells and mantras, you can also make a symbolic protective pentacle at any time – before an interview, meeting or psychic session or just at the beginning of a normal day. Simply draw it in the air, as described below.

1 Extend a finger and raise your right arm and extended finger to point straight above your head. You are about to draw the shape of a pentacle (see the shape in the picture below).

2 In one continuous line, without stopping, move your hand, finger still pointing, down as far as you can extend it to the side of your right thigh. Now continue moving up diagonally across your body to a point level with your left shoulder. Then move your hand straight across your body, level with your right shoulder, diagonally down to your left thigh. Now move it back up diagonally to join the point where you started from, above your head. Draw an imaginary circle around your invisible pentagram.

3 Turn around to face the opposite direction and repeat. Now turn to the left and repeat; then right and repeat. You have now repeated this move four times. To achieve the fifth (this is the magic number of the pentacle), close your eyes and imagine that you are drawing this pentacle in your Third Eye chakra.

A pentacle can help protect you psychically, even when created in invisible form.

Working with the chakras

Balancing, protecting and energizing your chakras is vital in any psychic work. This is because our chakras are the interface with our subtle body, the etheric and the astral bodies particularly (see page 32) as well as a key vortex linking us to the subtle energy of the universe itself. Chakra means "wheel" and most Eastern spiritual traditions use the chakras as the basis for self-healing, for healing others and for spiritual development.

There are seven main chakras located along the spine and many minor ones around the hands, feet, elbows and knees. Work with the main ones first. By developing an awareness of these threshold energy fields in yourself, you will also begin to sense other people's chakras and heal them, too. Increase your own chakra awareness by working with each one in turn.

Base Chakra

This chakra is located at the base of the spine, centred between the last disc and the pubic bone at the front. Vibrating to the colour red, it is concerned with our sense of being grounded. It provides a firm base and sense of security and it controls the basic functioning needs of the body. If you have a feeble Base Chakra you'll feel spaced out and not in touch with the world. You'll feel threatened by other people or unable to get any project underway or finished.

Sacral Chakra

Located approximately a hand's breadth below the navel, the Sacral Chakra is concerned with your sex drive, creativity and emotional state. It vibrates to the colour orange. If this chakra is underactive, you'll have little confidence in your sexuality and be scared of getting close to

In most Eastern spiritual traditions, balancing the chakras is the key to good health and happiness.

anyone. You may have problems relating to other people and fear they just want you as a sexual object.

Solar Plexus Chakra

Situated between the navel and the breastbone, the third, or Solar Plexus, Chakra relates to the colour yellow and is the seat of personal power. Rather like having one's own inner sun, it gives us a strong ego, a sense of our personal character, individuality and will-power. If this chakra isn't shining, then we let others dominate us, feel afraid to express our personal opinions or worry about what others will think about us.

Heart Chakra

Situated behind the breastbone and in front of the spine, the Heart Chakra vibrates to the colours green and pink and is the centre of warm, loving feelings. This chakra is about true compassion, love and spirituality; it directs our ability for self-love, as well as toward giving and receiving love. This is also the chakra connecting body and mind with spirit. When this chakra is not fully functioning, you may be afraid of revealing your feelings for fear of getting hurt.

Throat Chakra

The Throat Chakra is, of course, located in the lower end of the throat and is the centre for thought, communication, music, speech and writing. Vibrating to the colour blue, when this chakra is out of balance, you may feel timid, not feel like saying much, resent other people who say whatever they like, misunderstand others or just be generally unable to express your thoughts.

Third Eye Chakra

Located in the centre of the brow, the Third Eye Chakra vibrates to the colour indigo and is concerned with inspiration, imagination and psychic ability. When this chakra is not balanced you may be blind to the truth, be non-assertive, afraid of success and indecisive. You may not have any psychic sense or trust your intuition.

Crown Chakra

Situated on the top of the head, this is the centre for true spirituality and enlightenment, vibrating to the colour violet. It allows for the inward flow of wisdom and brings the gift of cosmic consciousness. When this chakra is unbalanced there may be a constant sense of frustration, no spark of joy and a frustrated sense of meaninglessness about everything. Balancing energy in this chakra gives you the ability to open up to the cosmic consciousness and connect to the light of the universe flowing through all things.

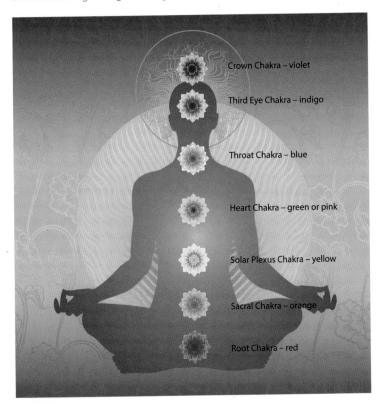

Crown Chakra – violet

Third Eye Chakra – indigo

Throat Chakra – blue

Heart Chakra – green or pink

Solar Plexus Chakra – yellow

Sacral Chakra – orange

Root Chakra – red

Strengthening the chakras

For any psychic work it is important that your chakras are all in good shape. Of course the Third Eye and Crown Chakras will be particularly useful, but the chakras must all be working in harmony to increase your psychic awareness and ensure you remain grounded and centred. You can then go on to do other meditation or visualization exercises, knowing that your chakras are balanced and empowering.

1 Find a quiet place, relax and sit cross-legged or lie down on the floor or on a bed. First, imagine your Base Chakra rooting you to the ground.

2 Hold your hands about 3in (7cm) away from the Base Chakra area, fingers pointing toward each other, palms inward. For a few moments meditate on this chakra area and the ideas, images and colours associated with it.

3 Now move your hands up to the Sacral Chakra area and do the same thing. Imagine the qualities and colours associated with this chakra.

4 Do the same with all your chakras. When you reach the Crown Chakra, place your hands above your head and imagine the energy of both your own spiritual Higher Self and that of the universe flowing through you. Now gently replace your hands in your lap.

5 Next, repeat the process, but without using your hands. Just concentrate on drawing the energy up from your Base Chakra, the colour red permeating your being. Then, as the energy moves up to the Sacral Chakra, the colour changes to orange, permeating your being and radiating beyond you.

6 Carry on with each colour until you come to the Third Eye Chakra and as the indigo colour fills you, know that your intuition and psychic powers are positive

qualities that will bring you life-changing happiness. Finally the violet colour of the Crown Chakra puts you in touch with universal energy.

7 Now, direct the powerful energy back down to the Solar Plexus Chakra, so that there is a circuit of energy flowing from the Sacral Chakra to the Crown Chakra, then back down again. Imagine this circuit of energy flowing around you whenever you feel vulnerable. This will strengthen not only your psychic powers but also your confidence and individuality.

Chakras and hormones

The chakras are linked to the glandular system of the body. When strengthening your chakras you are also strengthening your endocrine system, and, most importantly, the pineal gland. In 1969 research revealed that the pineal gland is physiologically linked to the hormone-producing glands (pineal, thyroid, thymus, pancreatic, adrenal, testicular/ovarian) which align exactly to the chakra points. The pineal gland releases melatonin, which influences rhythms of activity. Your physical, mental or emotional states are constantly changing, but these can be balanced by strengthening the chakra that corresponds to each gland, providing feedback to the pineal gland to maintain and regulate the body's natural circadian rhythms.

Creating your psychic sanctuary

Most people find that they need an imaginary "safe house" in which to perform their psychic work. This can be anything from a favourite room or a beautiful garden to a fantasy island, cave or temple. Some psychics imagine descending a staircase to reach a deeper level of consciousness corresponding to the theta and alpha brain waves (see page 48). One idea is to imagine being in a lighthouse looking across at the great cosmic sea of

Lighthouse sanctuary

Take this exercise slowly. The longer you take to use your imagination, the more you will get to know this personal place and the more it will become a welcome sanctuary. Once you have developed your left-brain skills, you will find that just by saying to yourself, "Go to the lighthouse" you'll instantly be there.

1 First, close your eyes. Concentrate on counting to 10 slowly, focusing on each number as you breathe in and out slowly to relax. Don't let any other thoughts come into your mind – if they do, go back to number one and start counting again.

2 Next, count down from 10 slowly, in time with your breathing. When you reach zero imagine stepping inside the doorway of the lighthouse. Slowly, begin to climb the steps to a room with a 360-degree view. In front of you is the sea, the beach

is to the left, the countryside is behind, the beach to the right and the sea, again, is straight in front. But this is no ordinary sea. It is the sea of cosmic consciousness.

3 Imagine that it is now dark out there, yet there are twinkling lights and other lighthouses in the distance; other people are heightening their psychic awareness – just like you. There is a seat where you can view the sea, where you can sit and relax, where your psychic sense begins to become aware.

consciousness. This corresponds to accessing the Third Eye Chakra and beyond to the Higher Self. This is a place where you can feel safe, and have concentration, mindfulness and an imaginery protective shield around you, so that you will not be swamped by your own sea of thoughts or those of others. The lighthouse symbolizes your own light and also lets other people know you are there. Try the lighthouse sanctuary first and see if it works for you. If not, use your imagination and discover another image that feels right.

4 Imagine sitting down in front of your bird's-eye view of the sea. Say to yourself, "I am now in the safety of the lighthouse; this is where I can do my best psychic work. If I want to be in this place, all I have to do is say, 'Go to the lighthouse', close my eyes, count down from 10 and I will be sitting here ready to get in touch with the cosmic sea."

For example, you might meet someone for the first time and have a vague hunch that they do not have your best interests at heart. To make sure your hunch is correct, imagine yourself in the lighthouse as you speak to them. Concentrate on the image in your mind and, as you do so, from your viewpoint onto the cosmic sea, you will see them as they truly are.

5 Now open your eyes. It is best to repeat this exercise every day for at least two weeks to make the image potent in your mind. Begin by doing this technique with your eyes closed, but also try to imagine being in the lighthouse with your eyes open. This is useful when you want to use your psychic powers in everyday life or when in direct contact with others.

Closing down the chakras

When you have finished any psychic work in your sanctuary, it is important to close down your chakras so that they are not exposed to the negative influence of other people you come across in real life.

Working down from the Crown Chakra to the Base Chakra at the bottom of the spine, imagine that the chakras are opened flowers and that now it is time to close them down to a bud again, as if for the night, one at a time. Alternatively, you can imagine that these seven chakras are light bulbs that you are switching off, one by one.

A Cambodian Siva head, clearly showing the Third Eye in the centre of the forehead. This is a mystical and esoteric concept representing a gate that leads to inner realms of higher consciousness.

Affirmations

Positive affirmations, when they are used consistently, change our internal language pattern and eventually transform any inner negativity we are holding on to into a positive attitude. This means that if you really want something and put complete faith in the outcome, having total belief in yourself, you will get it. Remember not to dwell on the things that you don't really want, only on the things that you do want.

Positive affirmations

Here are some affirmations that you can use to convince yourself and the universe that you merit success or happiness. Repeat the affirmations aloud and then write them down. Leave them in prominent places in your home, such as on the fridge door or the bathroom mirror, where you will see them every day. The more you repeat and think your affirmations, the more positive you become.

* I am filled with confidence and good intentions.
* I can transform my problem into opportunity.

* I love myself.
* I enjoy my positive thoughts and good feelings.
* I feel grounded and in the present moment.
* I know I will have success.
* I can cope with any situation.
* I am thankful for all the good things there are in my life.
* I create my own lifestyle.
* I will give value to others, as they will to me.
* I feel good about my unique self.
* Changing my beliefs changes my life (see page 104).

How positive can you be?

* When you read the positive affirmations on page 103 aloud do you really mean them? If the answer is "Yes", you're ready for some creative thinking. If the answer is "No", go back and reaffirm the affirmations until they feel truly authentic.

* Can you name at least five things you were grateful for today? If not – why not?

* When was the last time you smiled at a stranger?

* How often do you say "Good morning" to your plants or "Thanks for being there" to the trees? Respect nature and it will be good to you.

* When you're shopping, do you ever give up your place in the queue for someone else? If not, why not?

* Do you feel everything is against you or that you're fated? If "Yes", then the universe will, of course, oblige. If you feel everything is with you, then it will be.

* When was the last time you sent a card to just say, "I love you" to someone? Make a point of doing it today.

* Now finish the following phrases in your head and write them down. Hide the list away for a week. Then make another list without looking at the first and compare the two. Do the same thing again the following week and keep doing this for at least two months, if you can. You will discover that there are more things you can be positive about than you ever thought possible.

I am really pleased when I ...
I adore ...
I'm fascinated by ...
I enjoy ...
I am grateful for ...
I want ...
Warm feelings come to me when ...
I feel joy when ...
I intend to ...
My purpose is ...

The power of giving

In our relationship with the "world" we give or receive, go up or down, move toward or away. Equally, we must balance the desire for what we want by being grateful not only for what we will receive, but also appreciative of the success of other people. After all, what goes around, comes around. So practise the art of giving out good thoughts as well as thinking them about yourself.

* Resolve that every time you think of someone you think "good" things about them. Your mind may well struggle against this to begin with – "Hang on, I can't stand my boss ...". However the more you think kindly about them, the more positive energy you will be putting out to shape your own destiny.

* Try to practise the art of giving at least once a day, by giving someone a flower, a smile, a compliment, by sending a friendly email, giving praise or offering heart-felt sympathy.

* Receive nature's offerings, too. If it's raining, be glad for it; if there's no rain know that there is meaning behind it. If you were a farmer, a drought might threaten your livelihood, but it might also present a creative opportunity to decide to change your vocation, to act so that something better could come your way. Use this analogy for any problem you encounter.

Meditation

You have already experienced how visualization techniques (see pages 50–7) can help you enter a deepened state of consciousness, to access your psychic power. But you also need to learn how other meditation techniques can protect you from psychic negativity, both from within your own psyche and from outside sources, and help you to enter into a trance-like state of consciousness. Used by many Eastern spiritual traditions, particularly in Buddhism and yoga, learning meditation can help you focus on your outer goals and ambitions, and also bring you a deeper awareness of cosmic consciousness and your part in it.

The benefits of meditation

For thousands of years, meditation has been used as a way to calm the mind and achieve an altered state of consciousness to contact the spiritual realm. It can be used for:

* Lowering brain-wave frequency to the psychic alpha level
* Calming the mind and emotions
* Achieving a state of passive alertness
* Communicating from a higher level of consciousness
* Optimizing vital energy or Life Force
* Realizing the Higher Self/achieving mindfulness
* Having insight into the true nature of reality
* Focusing thoughts

* Boosting creativity
* Integrating the mind/body.

How to meditate

Repeat this meditation every day for 10 minutes, if you can, to focus and calm your mind.

1 Take 10 minutes out of the busyness of your life. Sit in a quiet place, either in a chair, with both feet on the floor, or cross-legged. Keep your back straight and hold your hands palm up on each thigh. Imagine a string attached to the top of your head, holding you up toward the sky.

2 Close your eyes. Notice your feet on the floor, your hands on your thighs, any sounds in the distance such as the fridge humming in the kitchen. Turn your attention to your body. Are you warm or cold, fidgeting or calm? Don't judge yourself or your feelings – just observe them. Don't reflect on your thoughts, just observe those that are going through your head, as if you are an observer outside yourself.

3 Now turn your attention to your breathing. As you breathe in, count one, two and so on. If your mind wanders, turn your attention back to your breathing and start at number one again. Take control of your mind, so that it does not babble and chatter distractingly. Focus on every breath and every number. Do this for about five minutes.

4 Now take a deep breath, stop counting and observe the stillness of your mind. Notice how peaceful you are for a few more minutes and reflect on being mindful in everything you do and say.

An alternative method to try is a meditation technique used in Transcendental Meditation, where instead of counting your breaths you constantly repeat a mantra in your mind to block out all thought. This can be a simple affirmation such as, "I will be better and more wise, giving and loving" or, "My psychic sense is awakening" or a more spiritual Buddhist mantra such as, "Om mani padme ohm."

Silent meditation

This meditation technique is practised by Zen Buddhists. It is not easy at first, but if you persevere for a few weeks you may arrive at a state where your right brain is in total control and your psychic powers can easily be accessed and activated. Follow the instructions below for a week, counting every in-breath in Step 3. The following week, count only on every other breath. In the third week, stop counting altogether. You will have an empty mind and yet be in an aware state, ready for psychic exploration. If you find thoughts keep babbling in your mind go back to the meditation on page 107 until you find the still, empty mind again. From this empty place, you will also find it easy to access the trance-like state needed to go to your psychic sanctuary (see pages 100–1).

1 Sit in a quiet place, cross-legged or on a chair, hands on knees and back straight. Start by focusing on an object in front of you – perhaps a candle. Be aware of sounds, your breathing and thoughts.

2 Now look at your left hand resting on your left thigh or knee. Stare at your hand and keep focusing on it without thinking about it or anything else. Focusing on your left hand activates your right brain and your thoughts will start to disappear from your mind.

3 Now turn your focus from your hand to the object and start counting your breaths as you inhale, from number one. This means you are using your left and right brain in tandem. Do this for 10 minutes. If you lose count, or left-brain thoughts take over, start again. With practice you will find you'll be working more with your right-brain mind than your left brain. This is when your right brain's psychic power will begin to develop to fruition.

The goal of meditation is to arrive at a state in which the mind is empty of all thought. Concentrating on a candle can help.

The benefits of visualization

How often have you imagined what you would like to happen in the future? Do you really "see" this future or do you just "think" it? Developing your visualization technique will mean you can take control of your destiny, because what you see is what you get (see pages 50–3). The benefits are:

* Learning to imagine visual images, which helps you to focus on your goals.

* Assisting meditation and altered states of consciousness.

* Quickly entering your psychic sanctuary (see pages 100–1) or protecting your subtle energy centre.

* Giving you psychic strength.

Dancing with the stars visualization

This exercise will take you further into the realms of your mind. Not only is it calming and strengthening for your psychic power, but it also offers a doorway to the sea of cosmic consciousness.

1 Relax, sit cross-legged or in a comfortable chair and close your eyes. Imagine that it is night time. There is no light pollution and there are no clouds in the sky. You begin to see stars – first the planets and the brighter stars that form the constellations. As you continue to gaze at the sky you see more and more pinpoints of light. Some are twinkling; others appear, then vanish. You see the odd shooting star, a satellite passing silently overhead and an airplane, too.

2 Now imagine you can dance among the stars. You are in the Milky Way, threading your way through the millions of stars and galaxies. The stars are your friends, your dance partners; they twinkle and light your way. Imagine you are their choreographer and you orchestrate the music of the spheres. You choose the vibrations of the universe; you select the steps that resonate to the harmonics of the cosmos. You are immeasurable, infinite – as the universe itself.

3 Now that you have danced a long way from home, begin to return. Follow the path back through the stars. Do the same dance, but now you are like the stars, forever changing but forever the same. The billions of stars in the sky are billions of souls – spirits that had once been on Earth. They bless you as you pass by; they wish you well and you blow kisses to each one as you dance the cosmic dance.

4 Now come back down to earth. Imagine yourself lying back on the grass in a summer garden, seeing all the stars in the sky from the ground. Beneath you is the earth, embracing you. You are grounded. Gaze a little longer at the night sky and the stars, knowing that they are part of you and that you have just met your infinite Higher Self.

The labyrinth

This exercise encourages you to realize that you can find your soul's purpose and follow your true path to success, so long as you have commitment to developing your psychic powers. It also shows that you can return to your "waking" state of consciousness at any time.

1 Relax and close your eyes. Imagine you are walking along a path by the edge of stream, which leads toward the base of a mountain and the entrance to a cave. Outside the cave is a sign that says, "The secret of your success lies within." At the heart of the labyrinth, deep inside the cave, is the secret, but no one has yet found their way back out.

2 You stop by the cave, curious; you want to know the secret. Inside, attached to the wall, is a ball of golden thread, infinite in length. You take the end that dangles there. As you walk into the cave you see over 20 pathways leading into the labyrinth. You know that whichever path you take will lead to your secret. You have the ball of golden thread and whichever path you take you can find your way out.

3 You plunge into the narrow passageway and immediately see others branching off to the left and right. As you walk deeper into the labyrinth, you let the golden thread fall on the ground behind you. You don't know where you are going, but then you see the sign, "The secret is here." You walk over and open a book that has no words in it. You stare at the book and know, intuitively, what your soul's purpose for you is as the words appear on the page.

4 You close the book and return through the labyrinth, following the golden thread back to the light of the day. Now you can open your eyes, knowing you have encountered the truth about your true vocation or life journey.

Spiritual and faith-healing

In spiritual and faith-healing, a healer acts as a conduit for the sacred energy of the universe. Spiritual healing is considered distinct from faith-healing. Spiritual healing is where the recipient passively receives healing, whereas in faith-healing both healer and recipient believe that the healing power comes from God or from some other divine source.

Valentine Greatrakes (1628–1666), famed Irish faith-healer.

Spiritual healing has been practised for thousands of years in most cultures, whether by shamans, priests or in healing temples, such as asclepieions of Ancient Greece. The most famous Greek healing temple of the god Asclepius was at Epidaurus in the northeastern Peloponnese. Another famous temple was located on the island of Kos, where Hippocrates, the legendary "father of medicine", is said to have commenced his career.

Universal energy

Healing energy is all around us. In essence it is "universal" – part of nature itself. It is available for everyone to use for the greatest good. Healers learn to use their ability to tap into this natural energy and pass it on to those who have not managed to heal themselves. In the East, this energy has been acknowledged for thousands of years as *chi* to the ancient Taoists and *prana* to the Vedic and Hindu cultures of India. The simplest way to describe it is as a Life Force. If you cannot visualize this Life Force, sometimes it is works to imagine the words "love" and "light".

Healers often use crystal pendulums to dowse the chakras or other areas of the body in order to find and correct imbalances.

Laying-on of hands

The healer usually scans the person's body with either the hands or with a dowsing pendulum, to sense unbalanced or blocked energy, or problems with the aura. Once they have tuned into these blocked areas, they act as a conduit for the energy to pass to the recipient's body, either through the laying-on of hands or by a contemporary version called "therapeutic touch". This is a technique that was developed in the United States in the 1960s by a professor of nursing, Dolores Kreiger, and a natural healer, Dora Kunz. The technique is widely recognized and used increasingly in the nursing profession as a complementary therapy.

A candlelight procession in Lourdes, France, world-famous centre of Christian healing.

The laying-on of hands (above) is a practice still popular in Christian churches around the world.

A medium heals a pilgrim (right) during Nino Fidencio celebrations in Mexico.

Faith-healing

Believing that a deity can heal you, or that the healer is channelling energy through God, became controversial in the 20th century, with many cases of fraudulent practice. In Christianity, faith-healing is also called "supernatural healing", "divine healing" and "miracle healing".

There are many references to faith-healing in the Bible, for example when Jesus tells his followers to cure sick people, raise up the dead, make lepers "clean" and expel demons. Healing, in this case, is interpreted as an act of faith. In Catholicism the most well-known faith-healer or miracle-maker is the apparition of the Blessed Virgin Mary known as "Our Lady of Lourdes" at the grotto of Lourdes in southwest France.

Well-known faith-healers include Smith Wigglesworth, a former English plumber turned evangelist, who is said to have lived a simple life and read nothing but the Bible. Wigglesworth travelled around the world preaching about Jesus and performing faith-healings. He claimed to have raised several people from the dead in Jesus' name at his meetings.

Today faith-healing is as popular as ever and regular meetings are held in many countries, attracting crowds – some even big enough to fill a stadium.

The Spiritualist Church

Members of the Spiritualist Church believe that, at death, the soul passes over to the spirit world. Mediums (see pages 248–51), rather than ordained priests, usually conduct the services and can offer not only contact with the spirits of the deceased to relatives, but also believe they have been given the gift of God's healing through their spirit guides. The church offers healing from either a medium or a minister and, similarly to all faith- and spiritual healing, this is usually performed through the laying of hands on the person's body or head.

Psychic healing

Psychic healing is the ability to cure other people using the psychic powers of the mind, whether through long-distance thought, prayer, healing affirmations, visualization, telepathy, psychometry or even psychokinesis. What distinguishes these approaches from other therapies – including alternative ones such as homeopathy, herbalism, acupuncture or self-healing – is that psychic healing does not involve any physical aids. From the scientist's perspective, there's little evidence to prove that the mind is capable of healing another person and the preferred explanation, in orthodox medicine, is that most of these cures must be based on suggestion and the body's natural ability to heal itself. The mind is simply a channel for the universal energy, as is the laying-on of hands.

Getting started

The best way to practise psychic healing is to carry it out daily. You don't have to actually lay your hands on anyone; you don't even have to know the person. You can practise just by sending out good-health thoughts, love and courage to a child you've read about in the newspaper who is recovering from an accident in hospital or a population affected by a natural disaster. Get into your right brain and send out your thoughts. This is a form of absent healing whereby the power of your mind simply physically channels the Life Force energy of the universe and directs it toward the person who needs it.

Using the Life Force

If you are physically with someone who needs healing, check the state of their aura by using the methods on page 132, or just use your hands to feel their chakras from a short distance from their body. Then all you need to do,

Psychic healing affirmations

When sending out good thoughts, it's useful to have a script, to begin with, to focus your mind. You can use these affirmations on yourself too:

✴ This healing energy will stay with you/me for as long as it takes to be healed.

✴ Love is all around you/me; it is there to benefit you/me.

✴ I believe in the Life Force that heals.

✴ The power of healing is mine to give to others/myself.

with utter belief in the power of the Life Force, is to send love and beneficial healing energy to that person, to trigger their own natural healing powers.

Cautious approach

Scientists and the medical profession are hugely suspicious of psychic, distant- and faith-healing. However, no harm can come of the method, as long as you do not try to "play doctor". It is important to use these forms of healing as complementary methods. Do not assume that they are the only way to heal someone else or yourself. If you take this approach, then the help you can offer by merely sending out good thoughts to someone may be enough to stir the healing process and shift the energy to help them. The more you practise sending beneficial messages, the more likely it will be that what goes around comes around. And that means the healing thoughts you send to others can work their way back to you too!

Esoteric healing

Alice Bailey (see page 62) was an influential writer on occult teachings, including esoteric healing, astrology, psychology and other philosophic and religious themes. The primary emphasis of esoteric healing is to heal the soul and Bailey believed that all disease is the result of inhibited soul life. It may be that when you perform any healing work, on yourself or on another, taking a holistic approach causes body, mind and soul to be healed simultaneously.

Energy healing

Other forms of psychic healing include those considered to be energy-centred such as Reiki and crystal healing. If, as Rupert Sheldrake suggests (see page 46) there is an invisible energy force around every living thing that we can manipulate, then – like the quantum fields theorized by Albert Einstein – these invisible energy fields are at the root of energy healing. The idea of the constant interchange of energy fields aligns with the Eastern approach to spiritual health and well-being and the universal energy, whether we call it the Life Force or "cosmic consciousness".

Reiki

In Reiki, healing energy is channelled through the practioner's hands. The word "Reiki" comes from two Japanese words – *rei* meaning universal higher power and *ki*, which is the equivalent to *chi*, the Life Force. The technique was developed by scholar Dr Mikao Usui as he meditated on a holy mountain in Japan. Legend has it that he sat beneath a sacred waterfall to purify his Crown Chakra and afterwards claimed he could heal others without losing his own energy. Reiki practitioners sometimes hold their hands a short distance over the client's chakras, or place them directly on the body. The universal energy is drawn in through the Throat Chakra and directed through the energy meridians of the client's body, depending on what needs to be healed. Reiki practitioners simultaneously replenish their own energy levels as they work.

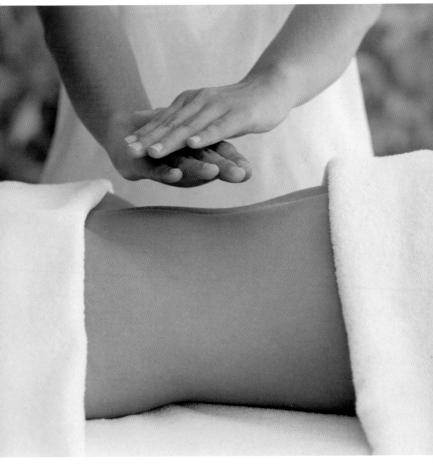

The powerful healing energy of the universe works through the practitioner to promote well-being for the client. This picture shows Reiki being carried out without physical contact.

Crystal-healing

Learning how to use crystals for healing yourself and others is simple. The flow of cosmic energy will work through you, either using real crystals in the physical presence of the person you are helping or by visualizing certain crystals and then sending crystal-healing energy via your psychic power.

Crystals are concentrated electromagnetic energy fields. Used as adornments throughout history, they invoke powerful healing energies and restore chakra balance. All crystals and gemstones vibrate to what is known as the "piezoelectric effect", discovered by French physicist and chemist, Pierre Curie. An electrical voltage passed across a crystal's face causes the crystal to expand and contract, thus creating a vibration. Any outside electromagnetic force, including that of humans, animals and so on, will have the same effect on the crystal, and in turn, the crystal's vibrational energy field is triggered to produce its own specific electromagnetic healing energy.

Crystals and chakras

If our chakras are unbalanced, we can use the vibrations of the crystals to harmonize, balance and stimulate their energies. There are crystals associated with each chakra (see chart opposite). When crystals are worn or carried, or placed on the specific chakras for healing purposes, they stimulate that chakra, so that both personal, spiritual and physical power is restored. When the chakras are functioning normally, each automatically draws in the particular energies needed from the universal energy field.

Visualize the colour and the crystal to send energy healing to someone else or to yourself. You can carry the appropriate one with you to balance and restore chakra energy during the course of the day. Alternatively, meditate while holding a specific crystal and feel the energy surge through you to align your mind with its healing powers.

Chakra correspondences

The vibrationary power of crystals can be used for all kinds of healing. Here are examples of how they can be used in conjunction with the chakras.

CHAKRA	CRYSTAL	MEANING
Base Chakra	Garnet	To enhance your sense of security, release you from fears and self-doubt and enable you to trust in yourself and others.
Sacral Chakra	Red agate	To enhance your ability to flow freely with your emotions and to feel and reach out to others, both sexually and creatively.
Solar Plexus Chakra	Topaz	To restore your outgoing nature and give you more self-respect and expressiveness. You will enjoy taking on new challenges and have a strong sense of personal power.
Heart Chakra	Rose quartz or pink tourmaline	Wearing or carrying these crystals will restore your compassion, empathy and sense of self-love.
Throat Chakra	Aquamarine	You will be musically or artistically inspired, your communication skills will improve and anything that you need to say will be said.
Third Eye Chakra	Amethyst	To restore your intuitive and psychic nature, as well as give you imaginative and visualization powers.
Crown Chakra	Clear quartz crystal	To give you the ability to open up to the cosmic consciousness and connect to the light of the universe flowing through all things.

Clearing negative energy

In many Eastern traditions, clearing negative energy is of profound importance, both in the home and in the landscape. When working with psychic power, you need to make sure that your home is free of the negative energy that comes from both the tangible world and the spiritual one. Perhaps long ago someone died in your home and their ghost still haunts the place, creating bad feelings. According to the Chinese tradition Feng Shui, arrows of naturally occurring unwelcome energy can attack a home or landscape. If the *chi*, or cosmic energy, flows freely in a spiralling or circular motion, or if there are plants, curves and the right balance of yin and yang, then negative energy will disperse.

If you have just moved or entered a house where you feel, intuitively, negativity in the air, or in one part of a house, then the following techniques will restore positive energy. One of the simplest ways to discover if there is negative energy is to dowse for it with a pendulum (see pages 139–41).

Burning

Light some small perfumed candles (sandalwood is excellent for warding off negative energy) and put them in as many different places (especially corners) as you can. Let them burn right down before you extinguish them. Alternatively, use incense. Lavender and jasmine are favourite fragrances, but sandalwood and other exotic perfumes all work well, too. Candles and incense burn away negative energy, giving space to good vibrations, and restore a balance of the electromagnetic field. Use colours that are important to your needs, such as: white for purification; red to empower your home and detract from the negative effects of high buildings or electric power cables near by; or yellow to send a lost soul or ghost on its way to the spirit world.

While the candles or incense are burning, you can also repeat mantras or affirmations to welcome good energy and tell the negative influence to be gone. "Smudging sticks" made of bundles of sage are also used for clearing negative energy. Take extreme care when you are working with fire – never leave lit candles, incense or smudging sticks unattended.

Clapping

Walk around the space and clap your hands briskly. Don't forget to clap in corners, under stairs, in cupboards and as high as you can above your head. Clap a drumbeat rhythm and the vibrant energy will soon shift any negativity.

Burning incense can be used to cleanse spaces of negative energy.

Sweeping

Literally, sweep away negative energy with a broom or a bunch of willow branches. Lift the broom into the air and sweep around windows or open doors, forcing the bad energy outside.

Communicating

Write a letter to the place in question and tell it your intentions. You are going to make beneficial changes and all negative energy will be gone. Then read the letter out loud inside each room. You can also do this psychically by meditating and concentrating on a mantra, such as, "All negative energy be gone; all negative energy be gone."

If you feel there are "bad" spirits lingering, you can communicate directly by stamping your feet in each room and saying, "Spirit be gone."

Clapping (left) clears the air.

Striking a Tibetan singing bowl (right) produces a delightful clear ringing tone that is perfect for cleansing poor atmospheres.

Bell-ringing

In your mind think good thoughts and feelings and then ring a bell or strike a Tibetan singing bowl as you walk around each room in turn. The sound waves will carry your thoughts to every part of the space. Bells can be replaced by any kind of musical instrument. You can beat a drum, play a violin, jangle or tap a tambourine, play a trumpet or sing your favourite song. Vibratory energy is the key, so if you prefer you can whistle, shout or even just jump up and down in every room.

Tibetan singing bowls are made up of seven different metals, which correspond to seven planetary energies. Tibetan Buddhists believe that these energies maintain not only the harmony of the universe but also realign harmony in the home. By ringing the bowl, the vibrations of the planetary energies are invoked and the space can be cleared of negative energy.

Aura-reading

The word "aura" comes from the Greek word meaning "breeze" or "air" – the "air" that emanates from the body. The aura is one of the systems of our subtle body energy (see pages 31–2), but it also interacts with the subtle energy of the universe. The aura connects us to the greater universal energy, of which we are all a part. When you meet someone for the first time, you might have an intuitive feeling about them. This is an unconscious awareness of the aura and how different, or similar, it is to your own. The human aura is the interface between the body and universal energy and is connected by the spiralling gateways of the chakras. The auric field is made up of vibrational colours, just like the chakras (see pages 94–7).

The source of auric energy

In many Eastern philosophies, the source of auric energy emanates from a place called the "hara", which is about halfway between the navel and the pubic bone. The auric field connects you not just to the chakras, but also to the nature of yourself, which is sited both in your gut instinct and the pivotal point just below the navel and also your soul. You are not simply your brain, detached from the rest of you; you are bound inextricably to all of yourself and the aura reveals that whole state. The sun itself has an aura, as does the earth and many other planets. The moon is said to have a special aura and on still, cloudless nights you can see its halo quite clearly.

In aura-imaging and Kirlian photography (see page 19), the aura can be made up of many combinations of colour, depending on the person's moods or state. Awareness of your own aura can be a positive source of self-healing, while reading other people's means you can help to improve their well-being, as well as know what to expect from someone when you first meet them.

Aura colour meanings

Dominant aura colours determine mood or personality. A good balance of colours is important for physical and emotional equilibrium. As moods and habits change so do auras and different colours may dominate at different times. Here is an interpretation for the nine colours when they are dominant in the aura.

COLOUR	KEYWORDS	MEANING
Red	Passionate, challenging, powerful	A predominantly red aura indicates a fiery enthusiasm for life and love and a strong ego.
Pink	Romantic, tender, idealistic	When pink is the main auric colour, loyalty, compassion and caring for others is important.
Orange	Creative, original, motivated	If your aura is vibrating orange, this indicates an independent mood or feelings of self-confidence.
Yellow	Intellectual, bright, optimistic	If yellow dominates, then good thoughts and happy feelings are radiating through your aura.
Dark green	Down to earth, ambitious, cautious	When green is dominating your aura, you're working hard and feeling good about your responsibilities.
Aquamarine	Freedom-loving, compassionate	Creative and romantic, aquamarine is the colour of genuine empathy with the world around you.
Turquoise	Inspirational, adventurous, explorative	When turquoise dominates, your happy-go-lucky energy enlightens others. You're in the mood to travel.
Blue	Sensitive, intuitive, emotional	If blue dominates, you are experiencing profound inner peace and you know exactly where you are going.
Lavender	Magical, imaginative, charismatic	You feel in touch with the world of magic and the supernatural when lavender dominates your aura.
Violet	Visionary, spiritual, spontaneous	If violet dominates, you're going through a period of spiritual clarity and can connect to your Higher Self.

Does your aura need strengthening?

Awareness of your own aura is a positive source of self-healing. But what state is it in? Answer this questionnaire honestly, to see whether you need to strengthen your aura. Answer "Yes" or "No" to each of these statements. For every "Yes" score one point.

Y   N

❑   ❑   I always think people are staring at me.

❑   ❑   I prefer being with friends to being alone.

❑   ❑   I don't find it easy to say, "No".

❑   ❑   I have high expectations of others.

❑   ❑   I always attract people who end up hurting me.

❑   ❑   I have endless ideas, but can't seem to ground them.

❑   ❑   At parties I hide in the corner.

❑   ❑   I get jealous if my partner looks at someone else.

❑   ❑   I get cross when I'm stuck in a traffic jam.

YOUR SCORE

★ 8–9: Your aura needs a few weeks of nurturing and strengthening.

★ 5–7: You need to do a little work on your aura.

★ 3–4: Your aura is in good shape – keep it that way.

★ 1–2: Your aura is vibrant – take good care of it.

How to nurture your aura

One of the best ways to look after your aura is to sit quietly every day and say to yourself, "This is who I am and every colour radiates harmoniously from me." But first you might need to strengthen your aura and protect yourself from outer negative energy.

1 Hold a piece of white quartz crystal in each hand. Sit comfortably and breathe deeply and slowly.

2 Focus on your hands and the power of the crystal energy coming through them. Feel the energy permeate your whole body and then emanate through your physical body and into your auric field.

3 Concentrate on this merging and replenishing of spiritual energy for several minutes to strengthen your aura.

4 Make a daily affirmation when meditating, such as, "I love my aura because I love myself."

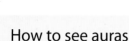

How to see auras

Seeing auras depends on how receptive you are to opening your sixth sense, and using your sense of sight as a conduit for seeing auras. They can be sensed in other ways, such as via gut feeling, smell, sound and touch. If you learn to amalgate your ordinary sense of sight with your psychic one you may be able to see auras. Here are two ways to start:

CANDLE AURA

1 Sit in a quiet, darkened room and breathe rhythmically and deeply. Light a candle and place it in front of you on a table. Concentrate on the candle flame and watch it flicker and sizzle. Make sure there are no draughts in the room and try not to breathe on the candle. The stiller the flame is, the better.

2 Focus solely on the flame and you will begin to see a glow around it in your peripheral vision. Imagine all the colours of the aura around the candle.

ONION-SHAPED LENS

1 Find a friend to be guinea pig. Begin by practising the "onion-shaped lens" by holding your hands in front of you at arm's length and positioning your fingers and thumbs to make an onion-shaped hole.

2 Ask your friend to stand in front of a white wall or unpatterned background. Raise your hands in the onion-shaped lens and imagine that it is a camera lens centred on your friend's body. Hold this position for a few minutes and concentrate on the image of your friend as you quieten your mind.

3 Gradually part your hands, but carry on concentrating on the same area of your friend's body that you focused on with the onion-shaped lens. Do not look at your hands as they move slowly apart. As you move your hands, you may find that you begin to see the aura around your friend's body – just for a moment. With some practice you will see more.

SEEING YOUR OWN AURA

1 Sit in a darkened room in front of a mirror about 2–3ft (60–90cm) away from you. Place a lighted candle on a flat surface behind you – you shouldn't be able to see it reflected in the mirror, but it should create a glow behind your body and head as you stare into the mirror.

2 Relax and for a moment close your eyes and go to your psychic sanctuary (see pages 100–1). Empty your mind of all thoughts and stare straight into the reflection of your own eyes. You will become aware of the candle glow behind you. Soon you will see the colours of your aura lit up by the candle. Remember, you may only see the candle glow at first and the process does take practice. The image shape and aura colours will change with your mood.

3 Once you have experienced seeing your aura with the candle, try repeating the exercise without the candle – you will see the radiance of your aura in your peripheral vision.

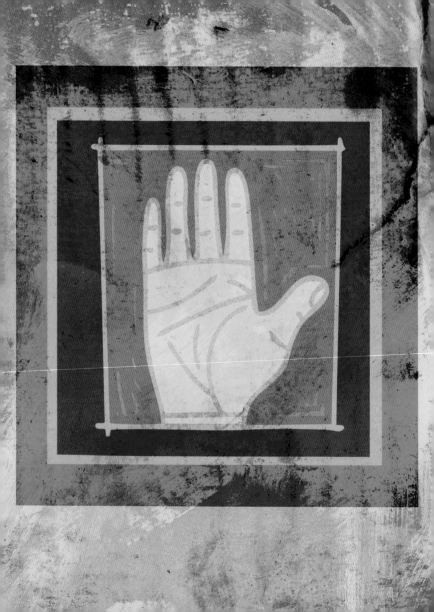

chapter 4

Divination

From a Latin word meaning "to be inspired by the gods",
"divination" is all about interpreting signs, patterns and
symbols to discover an answer to a question, gain deeper
insight into the nature of events or determine the future.
These methods not only rely on the psychic powers within,
but use various tools or systems for easier access to the
spiritual world. There are many ways of divining, such as
casting animal bones, gazing up at the clouds or searching
for patterns in water. More traditional forms of divination
include dowsing and scrying, as well as using Tarot cards
and runes. Get in touch with the power within you using
your favourite divination method and tap into the universal
energy that flows through all things.

Dowsing

The art of dowsing has been recorded as far back as the Ancient Greek era, when the sacred priestess of the Delphic Oracle, the Pythia, held out a forked wooden rod and recited magical incantations to hear the secret prophecies transmitted through vibrations from the infamous underground serpent (see also pages 12 and 13). Dowsing has also been known as "water-witching" or divining and the word can be identified with the old English *dewsys* (goddess) and *rhodl* (tree branch), but it is commonly thought to originate in the Middle German *duschen*, to strike.

Tools for dowsing

Dowsing rods are used for locating underground water, buried ores, metals and oil, and ley lines without using a scientific instrument, while pendulums, usually crystal or polished metal, are also used for occult predictions or decision-making.

The dowsing pendulum has been used for thousands of years as a "magical" device to reveal secret desires, find lost objects, determine the sex of unborn children and choose dates for special events. In Ancient Egypt it was used to decide on the best place to grow crops, while Romans were condemned for using it to plot against the emperor Caligula. In the 1st century CE, Roman scholar Mercellinus described how a ring hanging on a thread was swung around the circumference of an alphabetical circle, arriving at different letters to spell out answers to questions.

How does dowsing work?

Dowsing rods and pendulums are said to be a bridge between the cosmic consciousness and the diviner, who interprets the messages that contain

A woodcut (above), made in 1556, shows dowsing being used in mining activities.

This print (left) demonstrates one way of holding a dowsing rod (1762). Such rods were usually made from hazel, willow or trees indigenous to the area, and were used to find water and missing objects.

knowledge transmitted direct to the diviner from the cosmos. It is also believed that some people have an innate sensitivity to changes in the magnetic field, particularly when finding water or discovering lost objects.

When you begin to dowse, cosmic energy patterns permeate your unconscious mind and make the muscles of the hand holding the rod or pendulum react without you realizing it. This is called the "ideomotor

Using a pendulum, you can dowse Tarot cards to choose which ones to use in a layout, rather than randomly picking them from a deck.

response". The pendulum or rod simply amplifies these tiny, unconscious and involuntary movements.

A pendulum or rod enables you to tap into hidden inner knowledge. Whatever questions you ask, the answers come from the universal energy through your own unconscious mind. The best results occur when you remain completely objective; remember that if you ask questions about yourself or about finding a lost object, the pendulum or rod may be influenced by your wishful thinking. On top of this, emotional involvement with the question can often override the true response. So it's important to be honest with yourself when you are framing your questions.

The benefits of pendulum-dowsing

You can use the pendulum to answer virtually any question or to discover lost objects, people or future potential. The only other accessory you need is belief in your own power. Pendulums can help you:

* Find lost objects
* Confirm personal decision-making
* Select a potential partner
* Understand your unconscious desires
* Answer yes/no questions about the future
* Evaluate a situation or a person.

Choosing a pendulum

There are many different styles of pendulum, particularly crystal ones, which carry their own natural energy. Opt for the one you like for its look and its weight when suspended between finger and thumb. Round, cylindrical or spherical shapes are best because they are symmetrical. There are four main types of pendulum shape. The "Mermet" has a top that unscrews to reveal a cavity for placing a sample of what you are looking for. The other types are the pyramid, cylinder and faceted crystals. You can make your own pendulum by using a heavy ring suspended on a piece of thread.

Dowsing with a pendulum

Make sure that your body is relaxed and your mind stilled, and that you are open to the universal energy. Take several deep breaths before you start. If you have never used a pendulum before it might take a while before it responds. So be patient. The pendulum might just move a tiny bit at first, but it will eventually begin to move more strongly. Sometimes you might have to try several times before you get a reaction. The pendulum will work more fluidly if you remain open, imaginative and willing to trust in the unconscious energies flowing through you.

The way you frame questions is important. Don't ask, "Should I go out with John or Michael?" The pendulum only answers, "Yes", "No", "I don't know" or "Ask again". You can ask, "Does John love me?" or, "Will it be a sunny day on Saturday". You can also ask, "Am I really happy in this relationship?" or "If I left the country to start a new life would I be miserable?" These questions all have possible "Yes", "No" answers. Do not move your hand, arm or wrist while pendulum-dowsing.

1 For your first dowsing session, try sitting at a table and rest your elbow lightly on it. Alternatively, stand with your arm almost extended over the place you wish to dowse. Hold the end of the thread or chain of your pendulum between your thumb and first finger, using very little pressure, in a relaxed manner. The pendulum should be hanging about 12in (30cm) in front of you. If you are sitting, make sure your elbow is the only point of contact with the table. If you are standing, bend your arm at an angle of 90 degrees so that your forearm is parallel with the ground. Make sure your legs or feet are not crossed; this blocks the energy flow.

2 Deliberately swing the pendulum in gentle circles, just to get used to the feel of it. Experiment with the length of thread

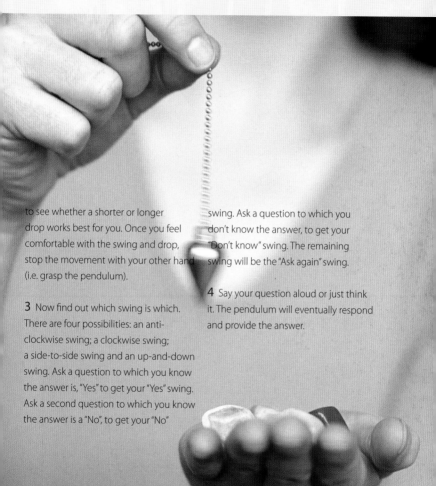

to see whether a shorter or longer drop works best for you. Once you feel comfortable with the swing and drop, stop the movement with your other hand (i.e. grasp the pendulum).

3 Now find out which swing is which. There are four possibilities: an anti-clockwise swing; a clockwise swing; a side-to-side swing and an up-and-down swing. Ask a question to which you know the answer is, "Yes" to get your "Yes" swing. Ask a second question to which you know the answer is a "No", to get your "No"

swing. Ask a question to which you don't know the answer, to get your "Don't know" swing. The remaining swing will be the "Ask again" swing.

4 Say your question aloud or just think it. The pendulum will eventually respond and provide the answer.

Three divination methods

These three different forms of divination (scrying, tea-leaf reading and ceromancy) employ a similar method of interpreting symbols or reading patterns that correspond to an issue or a question.

Edward Kelly became notorious at the end of the 16th century for scrying sessions in which he contacted angels and other spirits, apparently in attempts at political manipulation.

Scrying

"Scrying" derives from an old English word *descry*, which means "to dimly make out" or "to reveal" and has the same Latin root as "describe". Originally, scrying involved gazing at a flat, shiny surface such as a mirror or a bowl of water, interpreting the symbols or patterns to determine the future. One of the most famous scryers was Elizabethan magician Dr John Dee's accomplice, Edward Kelly, who used a special black-backed mirror.

Tools

Although scrying is associated mostly with crystal balls, any clear, shiny crystals or stones, glass objects, mirrors or bowls of water can be used. The Ancient Egyptians scryed with bowls of ink or blood, while in Persian mythology, the Cup of Jamshid contained an elixir of immortality in which scryers could see the seven layers of the universe.

The scrying process

The scryer, or seer, usually enters a trance-like state and freely associates the thoughts and visions that come to them through the interpretation of the

Visions of truth

Be relaxed, calm and ready to focus and take your time with this exercise. Scrying may not be as immediate as pendulum-dowsing; you have to engage your imagination and let it guide you to use your intuition. This is a great way to stimulate your imagination and power of concentration, both essential for psychic development. Carry out this exercise in a darkened room. Whatever happens, don't rush and expect instant results. You will be surprised at how accurate and revealing scrying can be.

Scrying using a crystal ball became a popular subject for 19th-century romantic art such as this detail from a work by English painter John W. Waterhouse (1849–1917).

1 Choose either a mirror, bowl of water, crystal ball or a white quartz crystal. Have a piece of paper or your psychic journal beside you. Sit quietly before the object and go gently into your psychic sanctuary using the technique outlined on pages 100–1.

2 Ask yourself a simple question; something that you don't know the answer to. For example, you can be quite general with a question such as, "What kind of day am I going to have?" Or, be

more specific with, for example, "Will my boss be in a good mood today?"

3 Gaze at the scrying object and when you see any shapes or patterns emerge, as shadows, ripples, shapes made by the light and so on, either note them down or draw them on paper. If other images come into your mind, write these down. You might see "nothing" but sense a feeling about the response. Make a note of this, too.

ripples or refractive qualities of light in water. They then use these to create a relevant story and suggest the outcome of future events.

Scrying helps you to develop your psychic imagination. Now that you have become accustomed to using visualization techniques to develop your Third Eye (see page 98), you can look for symbols or patterns to interpret. You may either literally "see" a vision or intuit it, or images and words will start to flow through your mind. If you start by saying these words aloud, you will begin to realize how you can interpret such psychic data into answers to any question.

Reading the leaves

This exercise shows how to use tea to access the power of the universe. Most tea-leaf readers consider the patterns nearest the rim to be concerned with the very near future, while those at the bottom of the cup are concerned with the more distant future. So if you ask the question, "When will I get news of the job interview?", the leaves near the rim indicate you'll do so that very morning, while leaves near the bottom of the cup indicate the evening or the next day.

1 First calm your body and mind. Make yourself a pot of tea with loose tea leaves. Don't use a strainer. While drinking your tea, think of your question. Start by trying a simple one.

2 When there is barely any liquid left in the cup, turn it sharply anti-clockwise three times, cover it with the saucer and then invert cup and saucer to let the liquid drain off into the saucer. Then pick up the cup and see what shapes or patterns emerge. Working in a spiral around the inside of the cup, begin to note patterns or shapes that emerge.

Tea-leaf reading

"Tasseomancy" is the interpretation of patterns in tea leaves, coffee grounds or wine sediments. It derives from the French word *tasse,* meaning cup (from the Arabic, *tassa*) and from *manteia,* the Ancient Greek word for divination. By studying patterns, the reader interprets the future. In traditional cultures there are usually specific meanings for certain symbols not necessarily coinciding with the symbolic language of dreams or astrology. It is perhaps better to interpret the picture revealed via your own sixth sense than trying to navigate your way through a maze of different symbolic interpretations.

In this tea-leaf reading, the leaves are all at the bottom of the cup, meaning that the reading is concerned with the distant future.

Possible bird shapes visible in cooling wax indicate that news is on its way.

Ceromancy

This is the art of divination achieved by dropping melted candle wax into a pan of cold water. The term "ceromancy" is also often used to describe divination by any drips or shapes formed on the side of a candle, or by observing how a candle flame burns. Try out the exercise below, but take care when you are working with dripping candle wax; it can burn.

Candle wax patterns

Seeing patterns in anything, whether clouds or candles, is a way of divining the universe. This exercise combines observation with imagination.

1 Take two candles and tie them together with a scarlet ribbon.

2 Either place the candles upright in a bowl of cold water or hold them at an angle, so that the wax will drip directly onto the water. Now light them.

3 Interpret any shapes formed by the hot wax as it solidifies in the cold water. Some traditional interpretations of shapes are in the list (see right), but it is your own interpretation, both intuitive and spontaneous, that really counts.

INTERPRETATIONS OF WAX SHAPES

* **Bird:** news is coming
* **Chain:** go ahead with your plans
* **Circle or ring:** it's a time for reconciliation
* **Cross:** you are protected
* **Splayed fan:** a surprise is coming
* **Heart:** friendship becomes love
* **Moon:** money is on its way
* **Table:** an abundance of blessings for you and your family

Dream interpretation and prophecy

Much debated by neuroscientists and psychologists, dreams were historically considered to be mystical or an altered state of awareness. They have always been an inspiration for interpretation. "Lucid" dreaming, when the dreamer is aware of dreaming and has some control over the dream, is often linked to exceptional human and out-of-body experiences. This applies particularly to the flying dream, associated with astral projection.

In many indigenous cultures dreams played an important part in shamanic and ritual magic. Native Americans went into the wilderness at puberty to dream their future into being and to find their spirit guide. Australian Aborigines believe in Dreamtime, an alternative dimension as real as reality, and the Ancient Greeks built temples dedicated to incubating dreams that would then be interpreted the following day by a priest offering cures for any disease.

Meaning of dreams

Our dream world has always been mysterious, fascinating, inaccessible and sometimes horrifying. Freud's ground-breaking theory in the early 20th century suggested that dreams are a kind of wish fulfillment, manifesting according to our hidden desires. Jung followed this up with the idea that our dream world is as relevant to us as our waking one, its symbolic content having personal and collective meaning. The characters and even the objects or animals we encounter in a dream are usually aspects of ourselves, as well as being part of the archetypal collective dream.

Some ancient cultures, such as the Egyptians, believed that dreams allow us supernatural communication and are also a means of divine intervention. They thought that messages from the deities could only be unravelled by those with specific powers.

The biblical Joseph was one of the earliest recorded interpreters of dreams, while in the 2nd century CE Artemidorus of Daldis in Asia Minor wrote a comprehensive text about interpretating dreams to predict the future. He believed that the meaning of dreams often involved puns on words or images, and that an image could be understood by decoding it into its component words. Chinese sages were fascinated by dreaming and wondered if it was a state in which one was more awake than one was when actually awake. One ancient myth tells how a monk, Chuang Chou, dreamed that he was a butterfly. He fluttered about happily, pleased with the state he was in, knowing nothing about Chuang Chou. Eventually he awoke and found that he was Chuang Chou. But did Chuang dream that he was a butterfly, or was the butterfly dreaming that he was Chuang dreaming?

The dream-catcher has an important role in Native American tradition. Drawing on the symbolic strength of the hoop, the central web protects the sleeper from negative dreams, while allowing the positive ones to slip through. Meanwhile, the negative dreams caught in the web fade with the morning sun.

Dream interpretations

Here are some of the commonest dream themes and their contemporary interpretations.

BEING CHASED

This may indicate a tendency to run away from responsibilities and avoid issues. The person chasing you may also represent an aspect of yourself. The next time you have a similar dream, turn around and confront your pursuer. Ask them why they are chasing you. Or ask yourself what you are running away from.

FALLING

A dream about falling usually represents instability and anxiety. There is a desperate sense of being out of control. You may also be ashamed of something and have no sense of self-esteem.

FLYING

The ability to fly in dreams has been described as being similar to an out-of-body experience. If you are really enjoying the dream's scenery and flying with ease, this is a liberating dream. It also suggests that you are on top of a situation. If you are having trouble flying, you lack power and may be struggling to control your life.

TEETH

Dreams about teeth may feature them either falling out or crumbling. One theory is that such dreams reflect anxieties about appearance. Teeth also symbolize power. Are you lacking power in your current situation?

HOUSE

Dreams relating to a house often refer to various aspects of the self, with the rooms relating to facets of your personality. The attic represents your mind, spirituality and your connection to the Higher Self, while the basement is the storehouse of repressed or denied feelings and qualities.

CHIMNEY

This symbolizes warmth, tradition and family values, though it could represent the phallus. If the chimney is smoking, then it represents sexual release.

DOOR

New opportunities are presented in dreams about doors. If a door is closed or locked, something or someone seems to be blocking your progress.

THE SEA

This stands for your unconscious and the transition between your unconscious and consciousness. As with other water symbols, the sea represents emotions.

BEING LATE

To dream you are late for an appointment or haven't got enough time to do something is a sign of your fear that you can't trust yourself to do something. You have little self-esteem and don't feel ready to move on. Alternatively, you feel time is running out and you can't ever imagine having all the things you want.

WAITING ROOM

A waiting room can mean that you are incredibly patient and that it's worth remaining calm because you will achieve what you intend. However, if you feel edgy and distracted, or if the train never seems to arrive, you need to leave the waiting room and not let other people prevent you moving on.

WEDDING

You may be going through a period of growth and transition and are about to become more at peace with yourself. If you see a specific type of partner in your dream, it may be these are characteristics you need to incorporate to become happier. Dreaming of marrying someone you were once involved with implies you've finally accepted that the past is the past; you can look back without regrets. Dreaming of marrying someone and regretting it means you are currently in a situation you find difficult to get out of; you need to know what you want before you make any commitment.

(Continued overleaf)

SNAKE

Snakes in dreams can represent your enemies, the things you fear in daily life or your unconscious sexual longings. They can also symbolize your fear of sudden or unpredictable events that could be stopping you in your tracks or creating chaos in your life.

BEING STRANDED ON AN ISLAND

This represents your need for solitude. Alternatively it can symbolize the fact that you are distancing yourself from someone because you fear rejection.

SEEING AN EX-LOVER/CURRENT PARTNER IN THE DISTANCE

Seeing your ex-lover with someone else in a dream can indicate unresolved issues or a lack of real closure between you. Perhaps you are presently living a "repeat performance" and wish you could change the outcome, fearful that it might end like the past relationship. However, this dream can also symbolize you feeling unhappy with your current partner.

FALLING IN LOVE WITH AN EX

Meeting a former lover and falling in love with them again in a dream symbolizes that you miss aspects of that person or the relationship. Although they have moved on, you still hanker for them and wish you could turn back the clock.

SCHOOL AND EXAMS

Dreaming about going to school or retaking exams symbolizes the lessons you have not yet learned about life. But if you have recently overcome a work or relationship challenge successfully, dreaming of going to school means that the lessons you have learned are at last being put to good use.

CELEBRITIES

Meeting specific celebrities, or dreaming you are one, means that you idolize their status. You yearn for a glamorous lifestyle and believe it to be better than your own. Dreaming of celebrities means that you are not realizing your own potential or unique talents, and you need to learn not to confuse admiration with envy.

NAKEDNESS

Dreaming you are naked in public symbolizes feelings of being exposed and defenceless; trying to be something that you are not; or you are fearful of being ridiculed and disgraced. If you are in a new work environment or in a new relationship, you may fear others seeing through to your inner vulnerability.

ANIMALS

Dreaming about animals symbolizes your own primitive desires, drives and sexual nature, depending on the qualities of the particular animal. Most wild animals symbolize the untamed and uncivilized aspects of yourself, while favourite pets represent your softer side, often the gentle qualities in yourself that need to be nurtured. Fighting with an animal signifies you are rejecting or denying a more instinctual part of yourself.

Working with dreams

From the biblical prophets Daniel and St John the Divine to Edgar Cayce, Jean Dixon and Gordon Michael Scallion, numerous visionaries have described their dreams and made prophecies using them. Prophetic dreams are believed to be a form of psychic precognition in which a person can perceive information about places or events before they actually happen. A study showed that over 40 percent of people felt they had had a dream about something that later actually happened. Many others have found dreams a useful source of inspiration. Author Robert Louis Stevenson revealed that his novel *The Strange Case of Dr Jekyll and Mr Hyde* was conceived during a dream, while golfer Jack Nicklaus found a new technique for holding his golf club through a dream and Albert Einstein was inspired by a dream to develop his Theory of Relativity.

One way of working with dreams is to incubate a dream, as the Ancient Greeks did, by asking a question before you go to bed and hoping to have an answer by the morning. Write the question down in a dream journal, to focus your intention and affirm to yourself as you go to sleep. It is important to ask a positive, life-affirming question and also to realize that you are more likely to get symbolic answers than literal ones. For example, any people you know who come into your dreams are likely to be representative of aspects of yourself and are not really those people themselves. You may not get an instant response, so try this exercise out over a few nights. If you do not receive an answer, it may be that there isn't one.

The prophet Daniel receiving his book from God in a miniature from a 1364 manuscript of the Bible. Daniel was one of the many visionaries to have described their dreams.

Palmistry

The ancient art of reading character and destiny from the lines on the palm of your hand is known as "palmistry", but there are several other distinct areas of study involving the hands. Some diviners use the skin patterns, known as "dermatographics"; others the shape of the hand and fingers, called "chirognomy"; and some just the lines and marks, known as "chiromancy".

Every hand is different, just as we have unique fingerprints. Ancient cultures in India, China and Egypt practised forms of palmistry and its influence in the West dates back to about 1100BCE. The Greek physicians

Basic hand shapes

There are four basic hand shapes, which correspond to the four elements of earth, fire, air and water. This can give you a clue as to your main personality type and your long-term goal. Having more knowledge about your basic personality can help you to determine what kind of psychic skills it is best to develop. Look at the four hand shapes below and decide which one most closely resembles your own.

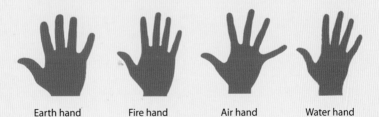

Earth hand   Fire hand   Air hand   Water hand

Hippocrates and Galen used palmistry as an aid to medicinal diagnosis and healing. The earliest-known manuscript to mention palmistry is the Digby Roll IV, written in English and dated to 1440.

Although considered to be heretical, palmistry eventually became popularized at the end of the 19th century by psychic performers such as Count Louis Harmon, who was commonly known as Cheiro the Irish Fortune-Teller, and it was thereafter treated more or less as a parlour game. Nowadays, palmistry is taken seriously once again and it is used not only to interpret the character and destiny of the individual but as a tool for the diagnosis of illness and disease.

A 19th-century Indian miniature showing palmistry in action.

Earth: the square or practical hand

HAND TYPE	KEYWORDS	CHARACTERISTICS	PSYCHIC POTENTIAL
Square palm with short fingers	Commonsense, practical ability	Down-to-earth and sensible, you view life with a hefty dose of realism and you can be quite sceptical about psychic power. You do well in the creative or practical arts and need plenty of challenges to keep you motivated. You are loving and loyal and take relationships seriously.	You are in touch with your senses, particularly the first five. Perhaps you can develop your sixth sense more easily if you first work on becoming more aware of sight and touch. Aura-reading and chakra work are essential in your psychic development. Keep up with visualization, commune with nature and feel at one with the universe through all the senses.

Fire: the energetic or intuitive hand

HAND TYPE	KEYWORDS	CHARACTERISTICS	PSYCHIC POTENTIAL
A long, oblong-shaped palm with medium-length fingers	Restless, animated	You just want to get on with life and love. Passionate and go-getting, you thrive on physical exercise and mental stimulation. You are confrontational and need challenges or adventures. Others envy your motivation and fast-paced career goals, but you are often too hasty to make the right decisions in love relationships.	You have a spontaneous psychic awareness. Sometimes you react quickly to intuition; at other times you ignore it. You have potential to develop your powers if you discipline yourself with meditation and work on your prophetic abilities. Keep a dream journal and develop psychic powers using crystals, scrying and the Tarot.

Air: the intellectual or balanced hand

HAND TYPE	KEYWORDS	CHARACTERISTICS	PSYCHIC POTENTIAL
A squarish palm with long slender fingers	Idealistic, communicative	You have a brilliant mind and are often inspired to communicate great thoughts. You live in your head, mostly from the left brain, so the psychic world, though fascinating, is frustrating because you try to rationalize it. You are logical and objective, but in love relationships are utterly romantic and often out of your depth.	You love learning, so learn a new technique every day. Take a light-hearted approach to your psychic powers and you'll find you begin to get in tune with your right brain and the intuitive world you secretly so admire. Dowsing and crystal-healing are fascinating ways to develop your power without taking you too far from reality.

Water: the sensitive or pointed hand

HAND TYPE	KEYWORDS	CHARACTERISTICS	PSYCHIC POTENTIAL
Narrow, slim or thin palm with long, slim fingers.	Sensitive, creative	You are extremely sensitive to your surroundings and are very aware of your psychic or intuitive powers. Romantic and dreamy, you're also unrealistic and life can seem so harsh that you're happier living in your imagination. Generous and kind to others, you can be moody: gregarious one day, a hermit the next.	You have lots of potential – you probably use your right brain more than your left. Because you're so sensitive, you can do well developing your skills in channelling or contacting spirits and guardian angels, but you need to work on protecting your subtle body energy.

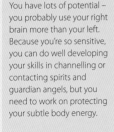

Basic palmistry lines and their meanings

Look at the illustration on the facing page. You'll see the three major lines marked on the hand. To get you started in palmistry, here are some brief interpretations of variations in the lines.

THE LIFE LINE

This line describes your vitality, your potential life journey and lifestyle.

* **The line curves widely into the middle of the palm.** You want to achieve great things and independence matters to you.
* **The line stays close to the thumb.** You're a home-lover – you just want a simple life.
* **The line veers away at the end, toward the outer wrist.** Travelling overseas will bring you success.
* **There are breaks in the line.** This signifies many changes in your life as cycles end and begin. Transformation and change will bring you wisdom and inner strength.
* **There is a double life line.** Often two lines run parallel to each other – one may be fainter than the other. You have a twin, guardian angel or you lead a double life.

THE HEART LINE

The heart line represents your relationships.

* **The line is strong and well developed** You will have many relationships, but usually happy ones.

* **A short or weak line** means you aren't in touch with your own feelings.
* **A line ending beneath your middle finger** refers to family and long-term commitments.
* **A line ending beneath your index finger** means you are free-spirited; you need friendship and space.
* **A line starting high up** means you are very self-conscious and self-critical.
* **A line starting low** means you are idealistic and often in love with love.

THE HEAD LINE

This line describes your intellect.

* **A strong and wide line** means you're willing to work hard for your living.
* **A faint or short line** means you can't make decisions.
* **A very long line** means you get lost in thought.
* **If the line runs straight across your palm** you are focused and controlled, but you need material security.
* **If the line dips down,** you're intuitive and imaginative and you work well in a creative environment.
* **A forked line** is a sign of being a brilliant writer or a successful communicator.

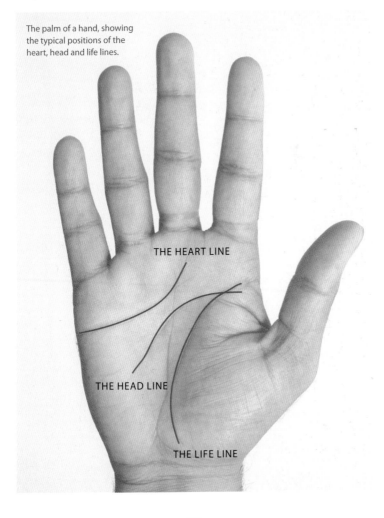

The palm of a hand, showing the typical positions of the heart, head and life lines.

THE HEART LINE

THE HEAD LINE

THE LIFE LINE

Numerology

Do you find that one number seems to mean something to you or crops up in your life more often than other numbers? Do you always live at number five in the row, or have five best friends, five favourite books or find that you see the number "5" everywhere you go? Numbers are basic symbols; they often occur in dreams, real life and seem to have a meaningful synchronicity to us. We can also use them to access the universal source of wisdom and psychic energy.

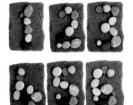

Based on the powerful vibrational frequency of numbers, numerology is an ancient system of divination used to find guidance for the future.

The numbers one to nine are the basis of numerology.

The early Taoist sages, Egyptians, Hebrews and Greeks used various systems of numbers for occult purposes. It was the Greek mathematician and philosopher Pythagoras who wrote in the 6th century BCE, "Numbers are the

Pythagorean alphabet code

Using the Pythagorean system, each letter of the alphabet is assigned a number. Any words can be analyzed using numerology once they have been coded in this way. Find your power numbers by adding up the numbers and reducing them to one digit (see page 164 for instructions).

1	2	3	4	5	6	7	8	9
A	B	C	D	E	F	G	H	I
J	K	L	M	N	O	P	Q	R
S	T	U	V	W	X	Y	Z	

first things of all nature." He believed that everything was symbolized by, or could be reduced to, a number. Numbers were central to everything in the cosmos and the primary numbers one to nine vibrate to certain frequencies throughout the universe. This concept of the "music of the spheres" described how the heavenly bodies worked together, each with a numerical value and harmonic vibration.

Basic meanings of the prime numbers

NUMBER	PLANET	GEMSTONE	KEY CONNECTIONS
1	Sun	Ruby	Summer, wholeness, unity, innovation, independence, creativity
2	Moon	Moonstone	Rhythm, dance, yin and yang, harmony, negotiation
3	Jupiter	Amethyst	Spring, growth, communication, positive thinking
4	Uranus	Green tourmaline	Strength, structure, stability, will-power
5	Mercury	Citrine	Autumn, creativity, adventure, travel, curiosity, versatility
6	Venus	Turquoise	Luxury, the home, love of service, teamwork, loyalty
7	Neptune	Aquamarine	Spirituality, mysticism, philosophy, music, art, dreams
8	Saturn	Black tourmaline	Winter, ambition, power, materialism, proficiency
9	Mars	Red coral	Universe, vision, humanitarianism, idealism, competitiveness, outspokenness

Destiny and personality numbers

We're going to see how your date of birth and your given name can reveal something about your goals and future potential. Your date of birth gives your "destiny number". You can't change this number, whether you like it or not. It reveals your life journey and the challenges on your way. It often indicates your true vocation and innate potential. Your name gives your "personality number". This describes your character, your qualities and the kind of relationships you may encounter.

HOW TO FIND YOUR DESTINY NUMBER

The more you fight against the vibrational energy of this number, the more challenges you will encounter. The best way to enjoy your life is to work with the corresponding ideas and vocational pathways symbolized by the number. This is the easiest number to calculate.

For example: If you were born **16 June 1984**, write down the numbers one by one (the month is represented by its position in the sequence 1–12) and then add them up.

1+6+6+1+9+8+4 = 35

Then reduce this number to one digit.

3+5= 8

So your destiny number is **8**

HOW TO FIND YOUR PERSONALITY NUMBER

Most of us don't use the whole of our given name in day-to-day life. If your name is Catherine Jane Smith, you may prefer to be known as Kate Smith or Cathy Smith, or you might have changed your name because you didn't like it. Or perhaps you have married and changed your surname. It's worth looking at both your formal, given name and its associated number and the name you like to be known by and the resultant number. We often change our name so that, unconsciously, we can alter our life in some way.

Look at the Pythagorean alphabet code (see page 162) and write down a number for each letter of your name. For example:

if your preferred name is Kate Smith, you'd write down:

2+1+2+5+1+4+9+2+8 = 34

Now reduce to one digit 3+4 = 7

So your personality number is **7**

CORRESPONDING MEANINGS

Armed with your personality and destiny numbers, you can now look at what they mean.

Destiny numbers: meanings

1 You are born to be a leader.
2 Choose a vocation in which you can negotiate.
3 Work in the media, as a writer or in the travel business.
4 You will do well in business.
5 You need adventure, travel or a sense of mission.
6 This number is great for any healing vocation you may choose.
7 Consider a psychic or spiritual career.
8 You need to be in a powerful role such as head of the company.
9 You are an idealist. You will have many career changes before you decide one is worth your devotion.

Personality numbers: meanings

1 Bright, sparkling and self-motivated, you're everyone's best friend.
2 Gentle and sensitive, you often take on too many problems.
3 Romantic and flirtatious, you take each day as it comes.
4 Being practical and good with finances means you're often the power behind the throne.
5 Impulsive and adaptable, you're a real risk-taker.
6 Protective and loyal, you have high standards at work and at home.
7 Dreamy and acutely sensitive to other people's moods, you're a born mystic.
8 Self-controlled and self-willed, you're dedicated to your own success.
9 Romantic, selfless and free-spirited, you live by your wits.

Destiny and personality numbers may conflict: a number 7 dreamer and a number 4 business leader seem incompatible, with tension between inner potential and outer comfort zone. Consider how tension can be resolved. Stepping out of your comfort zone could release time to make a success of those dreams.

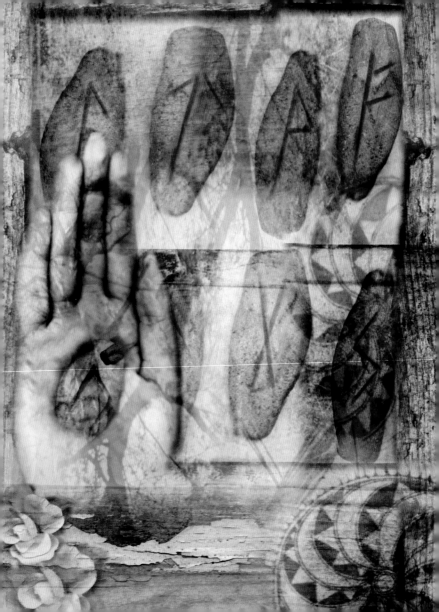

chapter 5

Tools for psychic powers

A psychic tool can serve as a bridge between everyday reality and all that lies beyond the veil of the tangible – whether understood as the spirit world or the domain of paranormal energies. Some divination tools, such as the Tarot, can also be used as a mirror for psychological self-discovery, but this chapter concentrates on deeper levels of experience. Even in such controversial terrain, however, the surprises often spring from our own hidden powers. It might seem as if a psychic tool is doing all the work, yet in fact it is demonstrating that there is more to your abilities than the mental and the physical. People are often drawn to the methods that work best for them: here is a selection to try out.

The Tarot

The Tarot is a visually exciting deck of 78 mystical cards, which has been used for centuries as a psychic tool. The deck is made up of 22 Major Arcana cards and 56 Minor Arcana cards, divided into four suits. One of the Tarot's greatest attractions is that every Major Arcana card is composed of vivid images that symbolize various archetypes, qualities, experiences, emotions and even people. The most popular decks, such as the Rider-Waite, have images for all the "pip", or Minor Arcana, cards, too. This enables you to not only draw on the "recognized" interpretations for each card, and feel secure in that knowledge when you are carrying out a reading, but also to use your intuition. The card reveals the energy of the moment and your psychological aspect, and allows you to dig deeper into the psychic world, tapping into the universal energy.

History of the Tarot

No one really knows how or where the Tarot began. Decks of mystical numbered cards existed in the Far East and in Egypt in ancient times. These may have caught the attention of travellers and crusaders, who brought back the idea to Europe before the Middle Ages. The first known set of Tarot appeared in the early 14th century in Italy, but the 18th-century French occultist Antoine Court de Gébelin claimed that the 22 Major Arcana were originally a set of Ancient Egyptian tablets of mystical wisdom, brought to Europe by the Magi. Whatever the case, in the late 19th century, the mystic and scholar Arthur Edward Waite developed, along with his colleague artist Pamela Coleman Smith, the well-known Rider-Waite deck, which is still favoured today in the English-speaking world. The 18th-century Marseilles deck is most popular in Europe.

The origins of Tarot cards in Europe are still swathed
in mystery. By the 16th century, fortune-telling
using a set of cards became fashionable throughout
the European courts as shown in this French
engraving from the 19th century.

How the Tarot works

As with any divinatory tool, the Tarot is given its random power in the moment, whether through a choice of words, a personal insight or intuition or a link to the universal energy that pervades everything simultaneously. The Tarot works according to the ancient belief that everything in the universe is connected, whether this is shown in the patterns in a tea cup, the card turned at the same moment as someone crossing the road or a butterfly flapping its wings in a distant jungle. Each event, experience or random shuffling of the cards is of that moment and its synchronicity – the inter-connecting factor between you, divine knowledge and future outcome.

The key

The key to using the Tarot is first to discard all your projections, your desires, your feelings or your judgments about the cards and to open yourself up to the universal energy, letting the card "speak" through you. For example, if you choose the Death card your immediate reaction might be to project negative thoughts onto it, seeing the card as "bad" and unwelcome. You judge the card according to your mood and say, "There must be bad things coming my/your way." However, if you draw on your intuitive skills, plus the interpretations given in this book, you will find that Death is very much about change and that the interpretation can promote acceptance of that change or some form of personal liberation.

The door

The Tarot carries a powerful symbolism. There is a message in every symbol and a meaning behind every image. Many of the images will stir vague recollections or ideas in your conscious mind; some you will identify with, while others will seem unimportant. The Tarot works because it holds all the secrets, the arcana of the universe, in the 78 cards of the deck. Each card in the Major and Minor Arcana – "Arcana" meaning "secrets" – is both a symbol of an archetypal quality and a clue to the answer to your question. Each card leads us to the very threshold of our unconscious and its interface with the universe. The Tarot, if you like, is a doorway to revealing everything that you want to know.

The mirror
The Tarot works because it is a mirror of yourself. When you shuffle the cards and begin to place them in a spread (see pages 182–3), your actions and choices represent aspects of yourself. The symbols you read will manifest "out there" in the apparent external world, but are also within your psychic self. Any reading is therefore tapping into both the universal energy, within and without, and your own inner being. Trust in both your own psychic power and the symbols you see before you.

Using the Tarot

Visualize the imagery of the key, the door and the mirror before you carry out a Tarot reading. Alternatively, repeat a simple mantra for a few moments such as, "This is key to opening the door to see all I need to know in the mirror of the universe." Remember that the universe always answers truthfully.

For the exercises in this book, which are an introduction to using the Tarot for psychic purposes, you need know only the brief key words and card interpretations given on pages 172–81. You can either divine directly from the illustrations of individual cards in this book or, if you want to try out the sample spreads suggested on pages 182–3, you will need to use your own deck. Choose one that has good pictorial images that you truly feel a connection with.

The Major Arcana

CARD AND NUMBER	KEYWORDS	MEANING
THE FOOL 0	Impulsive, eternal optimist, blind to the truth	Indicates a new beginning, or that a wild, irresponsible person is coming into your life. Watch out for leaping in at the deep end or of being too sure of yourself or of someone else.
THE MAGICIAN 1	Initiative, persuasion, wisdom, adapting to changing circumstances	This card means you can now bridge the gap between what you want and what you need. It is timely to adapt and juggle with ideas to find the right way forward.
THE HIGH PRIESTESS 2	Hidden feelings, trusting your intuition; the unconscious, feminine mystique	This card indicates it's time to delve into your own heart and trust what you find there. As a future card you will soon be enlightened about a problem, or a secret will be revealed.
THE EMPRESS 3	Abundance, sensual pleasure, progress, success	Time to create harmony in your relationships. This is a creative card and it promises that material wealth will come your way if you make an effort. In relationship issues it indicates sexual completion.

CARD AND NUMBER	KEYWORDS	MEANING
THE EMPEROR 4	Power, authority, leadership	This card often represents a male authority figure influential in your life. It also indicates insensitivity to others' feelings or the need to think rationally and not let your heart rule your head.
THE HIEROPHANT 5	Conforming, holding back, respect, tradition	A spiritual advisor can be of help in the future. As a future card it means you will soon be on the right spiritual path. Other people's beliefs may be of importance to your own.
THE LOVERS 6	Love, temptation, choice, commitment, completion	This is a complex card, but its most common meanings are: a choice in a love affair must be made; you're involved in a love triangle that needs resolving; love is coming your way.
THE CHARIOT 7	Perseverance, will-power, diligence	When you draw this card you're likely to meet someone who is motivated and means business, or that you can now stick to your guns, but should take care not to be pulled in two directions.

The Major Arcana (continued)

CARD AND NUMBER	KEYWORDS	MEANING
STRENGTH 8	Courage, facing reality; compassion	It's time to force an issue out into the open, or to stop others controlling you. Be prepared to forgive and forget. You now have the strength to face up to your faults and get in touch with your spiritual Higher Self.
THE HERMIT 9	Discretion, detachment, withdrawal	When you draw this card it's timely to retreat a little from the illusions of life. As a future card it means that you may fear revealing a secret or refuse to face the truth.
THE WHEEL OF FORTUNE 10	Inevitability, good timing, new cycle	This card symbolizes the cycles of the universe and your interaction with them showing how, if you take a chance rather than run and hide, you will overcome all obstacles.
JUSTICE 11	Fairness, harmony, compromise, legal matters	Right now objective thoughts are needed. As a future card it means that legal issues and settlements can be resolved. This card suggests that all is fair in love and war.

CARD AND NUMBER	KEYWORDS	MEANING
THE HANGED MAN 12	Transition, limbo, paradox, readjustment	A complex card, which often indicates we are sacrificing too much for someone else; or that it is time for readjustment and transition, however hard it feels to move on.
DEATH 13	Change, new beginnings, transformation	This card always represents the end of an old cycle or the start of a new one. This is a positive card and it implies it is timely to accept and embrace change rather than fear it.
TEMPERANCE 14	Self-control, merger, blending ideas	Moderate your desires or needs and your life becomes clearer. You will see the truth of your own psychic power. The emotional and sexual balance is good between you and a lover.
THE DEVIL 15	Sexual temptation, illusions, materialism	This card often indicates ignorance in relationships, perhaps confusing sex with love. As a future card it means that material issues will influence a new relationship.

The Major Arcana (continued)

CARD AND NUMBER	KEYWORDS	MEANING
THE TOWER 16	Unexpected events; disruption	It's timely to break down the old to herald the new. This may be through external disruption or a personal revelation, but a dramatic upheaval will change your life for the better.
THE STAR 17	Inspiration, ideal love, truth revealed	Your expectations may be high, but you are about to feel truly in touch with universal energy, which will allow you to navigate more positively through life.
THE MOON 18	Intuition, unrealistic dreams	This card is often a warning to you to not believe all you hear or see. It can indicate that you're deceiving yourself about a love affair and you must trust your intuition.
THE SUN 19	Communication, sharing, positive energy, creativity	A happy card, indicating all the success or happiness you're hoping for is coming your way. As a future card it means a playful romance or children will become important to you.

CARD AND NUMBER	KEYWORDS	MEANING
JUDGEMENT 20	Judgement, liberation, inner calling	This card is about dropping old values and accepting things the way they are. You may have to make decisions based on facts rather than on your instincts.
THE WORLD 21	Freedom, cosmic love	This is the ultimate spiritual blessing card. It promises freedom from fear and travel – both around the word and through the spiritual spheres. It is a card of the celebration of life. Time to enjoy!

The Fool, seen here with all the other Major Arcana cards, also represents you as you embark on your Tarot journey. Each card in the Major Arcana symbolizes a step toward spiritual enlightenment or psychological truth. The Fool, the only unnumbered card, must go on a quest to encounter the qualities or experiences of all the numbered Major Arcana, to realize that all the other cards are contained within him. This is you.

The Minor Arcana (Wands)

CARD	KEY MESSAGES
ACE OF WANDS	New beginnings, originality, fresh start; adventurous love and romance.
TWO OF WANDS	Feeling you have the whole world to conquer; having the courage to be different.
THREE OF WANDS	Instinctively knowing what is about to happen next; starting a journey.
FOUR OF WANDS	Exuberant love is coming your way; being freed from the chains of responsibility.
FIVE OF WANDS	Silly quarrels; feeling challenged, persecuted or frustrated by others.
SIX OF WANDS	Getting on your high horse; showing off, being the centre of attention.
SEVEN OF WANDS	Confident you can defend your views; gaining an advantage, winning.
EIGHT OF WANDS	Priorities up in the air; receiving an important message; taking action.
NINE OF WANDS	Being prepared for anything; worries about the future, over-cautious.
TEN OF WANDS	Overburdened, weary; it seems you're to blame; you can't think straight.
PAGE OF WANDS	Seductive admirer on the scene; feeling full of childlike energy.
KNIGHT OF WANDS	Unreliable lover or treacherous new romance; you feel daring and impatient.
QUEEN OF WANDS	Charismatic woman who knows what she wants is important to you.
KING OF WANDS	Powerful male figure will influence your life; feeling confident in yourself.

The Minor Arcana (Cups)

CARD	KEY MESSAGES
ACE OF CUPS	Self-expression; new romance; desire for a deeper commitment.
TWO OF CUPS	Sexual attraction; harmony and peace, reconciliation.
THREE OF CUPS	Social enjoyment, feeling on the same wavelength as friends/lovers.
FOUR OF CUPS	Unsure of anything and lacking confidence; feeling defensive, victimized.
FIVE OF CUPS	Regretting the past, wishing things were different; loss and disappointment.
SIX OF CUPS	Wishing you were a child again; meeting someone from the past.
SEVEN OF CUPS	Disorganized feelings; high expectations in love; careless attitude to love.
EIGHT OF CUPS	Realizing you have to move on; exploring a new perspective; sexual questing.
NINE OF CUPS	Sexual satisfaction; self-indulgent, lazy, concerned only with yourself.
TEN OF CUPS	Family means everything; promise of peace and happiness.
PAGE OF CUPS	Younger, imaginative lover.
KNIGHT OF CUPS	Knight in shining armour, unrealistic lover; being emotionally rescued.
QUEEN OF CUPS	Emotional contentment; compassionate lover.
KING OF CUPS	Wise friend; an older lover; accepting your feelings.

The Minor Arcana (Swords)

CARD	KEY MESSAGES
ACE OF SWORDS	Logical and facing the truth; analyzing someone's motives.
TWO OF SWORDS	Being blind to the truth; ignoring other people; denying your feelings.
THREE OF SWORDS	Feeling wounded or let down; jealous imaginings; lost love.
FOUR OF SWORDS	Taking a break to re-evaluate your life; repose, contemplation, meditation.
FIVE OF SWORDS	Dishonourable behaviour; winning a losing battle; hostility.
SIX OF SWORDS	Looking forward to better times; leaving the past behind, no regrets.
SEVEN OF SWORDS	Keeping things to yourself; manipulative or cheating friends/lovers.
EIGHT OF SWORDS	Trapped by a situation; floundering in feelings, refusing to listen.
NINE OF SWORDS	Sleepless nights; regretting your choices; wishing you were someone else.
TEN OF SWORDS	Feeling sorry for yourself, victimized.
PAGE OF SWORDS	A young-at-heart friend helps you out; youthful ideas.
KNIGHT OF SWORDS	Insensitive lover; brash colleagues; cut off from your feelings.
QUEEN OF SWORDS	Judging others too quickly; finding fault; hyper-critical woman.
KING OF SWORDS	Direct action needed; getting to grips with a situation.

The Minor Arcana (Pentacles)

CARD	KEY MESSAGES
ACE OF PENTACLES	Accomplished and down-to-earth success.
TWO OF PENTACLES	Being able to juggle ideas and actions.
THREE OF PENTACLES	Team spirit and cooperation needed.
FOUR OF PENTACLES	Being possessive or penny-pinching, wanting it all.
FIVE OF PENTACLES	Feeling left out in the cold; spiritual separation.
SIX OF PENTACLES	Compromising to gain power; approval-seeker.
SEVEN OF PENTACLES	Seeing good results for your efforts; taking a break from hard work.
EIGHT OF PENTACLES	Dedicated to your talents; perseverance pays off.
NINE OF PENTACLES	Enjoying the finer pleasures of life; deserving success.
TEN OF PENTACLES	Emotional and spiritual well-being; security.
PAGE OF PENTACLES	Financial messenger with good news.
KNIGHT OF PENTACLES	Cautious person in love; emotional detachment.
QUEEN OF PENTACLES	Nurturing, warm-hearted lover; resources on the up.
KING OF PENTACLES	Wealthy in spirit and soul; material riches to come.

Laying out Tarot spreads

There are many spreads (card layouts) you can use for different types of readings. Some people like to delve into their own psyche and learn more about themselves; others use the Tarot to reach for profound spiritual truths or to divine the future. For example, you may want to find out what the year ahead holds, so you simply lay out one card for each month of the year, in a line of 12, before interpreting the card for each month. Here are some simple spreads to try – they can be used for other people, but if you're a beginner practise on yourself first. The first two spreads explore the past, present and future and advice from your guardian angel, while the Mystic Seven spread is for general inspiration.

1 Find a quiet place, relax, close your eyes and enter your psychic sanctuary (see pages 100–1).

2 Shuffle the cards, cut three times and place the deck face down.

3 Turn over one card at a time and place it in the designated position, face up.

THE "YOU, NOW" SPREAD

1 You, Now (e.g. The Lovers) Love is a big issue for you.

2 The Past (e.g. Ace of Swords) You always believed you could be rational, rather than being torn apart by feelings.

3 The Future (e.g. The Hermit) You will need to find space alone to discover the truth.

GUARDIAN ANGEL SPREAD

1 **Your spiritual quest** (e.g. Ten of Wands)
   To be in touch with your Higher Self.
2 **What's stopping you?** (e.g. The Empress)
   Too many earthly temptations.
3 **Your angel's advice** (e.g. The Hierophant)
   Join a group with a specific belief system.
   Be self-disciplined, not self-indulgent.

MYSTIC SEVEN SPREAD

1 **Current situation** (e.g. Page of Pentacles)
You are dreaming of financial success.
2 **Obstacles** (e.g. The Fool) Your ideals are
impractical.
3 **What you need to learn** (e.g. Ace of
Pentacles) Organization skills.
4 **What you need to relinquish** (e.g. King of
Swords) Parental values that aren't your own.
5 **Who will help you?** (e.g. Five of Cups)
Someone who has lost all they had.
6 **The next step** (e.g. Temperance) Modify plans
and develop spiritual and material values.
7 **The outcome** (e.g. Three of Cups) Working with
others will help you to achieve your goals.

Psychometry

This is a skill that involves handling objects to discover, through psychic means, information about people and places connected with them. Using the sixth sense and opening yourself to the universal energy, you can learn to read the energy patterns that have been left in and around these objects. It's a bit like leaving a footprint in the sand, though of course the subtle body energies that linger around objects and places are invisible.

Rings and other jewelry, photos, clothes and similar possessions are usually used in psychometry as these are the things that are most personal to us. You can use the technique to discover the whereabouts of someone, as well as information about the future and the past.

How psychometry works

When we handle or touch something, we leave a spiritual "footprint" attached to that object. However, our body's subtle energy field will be mingling with the old energy fields left by other people, so the object may reveal things that are not relevant to us or to the querent. When you "tune in", using psychometry, you have to learn to adjust the energy to the right frequency, through your intuition, to interpret the spiritual footprints you discover. Using psychometry is a bit like listening to a radio where several frequencies are battling it out to be heard at once.

We leave psychic "footprints" everywhere we go, caused by our subtle body energies or the energy of an event or a trauma. Many personal objects carry our imprint, ready to be interpreted by the psychometrist.

Psychometry in practice

The art of reading spiritual footprints involves using both the left (rational) and right (intuitive) parts of your mind and getting them working in tandem. In much psychic work left-brain thoughts often get in the way. But in psychometry, we need to feed our right-brain intuitive processing with some left-brain facts about what we see, feel, smell or hear.

We often sense people's moods and this can make us feel the same way ourselves. Approach a psychometry reading in a similar way. Don't try too hard to begin with; it is the openness of your mind that is most important. Practise in other people's houses. Touch walls, furniture and personal possessions and see what you feel or sense. Psyching out energy from houses can be exciting – you may be picking up spiritual footprints from long ago. It takes time to be a good psychometrist, so be patient.

Our journey through life is marked by our spiritual footprints, just as footprints in the sand reveal that someone has passed that way.

Develop your psychometric powers

The first exercise introduces you to noting spiritual footprints and using the imagination to bring the past to life. In the second exercise you use objects and/or places to spark your intuition.

SENSING A SPIRITUAL FOOTPRINT

1 Sit in a quiet place. Look at a book. With your left brain you know it has a name, a shape, a texture and a smell. Think clearly about these. Now invent a story around the book and someone who might have read the book in the past. Do this until your right brain takes over and you start to "feel" the energy of the book and its absent reader.

2 Don't open the book, just hold it and imagine reading it. Retell an incident that occurred in the book. It may be a fictitious idea that jumps into your mind or something you are suddenly sure you remember reading. By doing this, you are activating the psychic energy of the person who used the book. Their spiritual footprint is not just invisibly encoded in the book itself, but is now being brought to life by your mind.

TUNING INTO AN OBJECT'S PAST ENERGIES

1 Ask a friend to help you practise in a quiet place, where you can focus, relax and visualize from your psychic sanctuary (see pages 100–1).

2 Ask your friend to give you a personal object, such as a watch, ring or piece of clothing. Take the object in your hands, close them around it and shut your eyes.

3 After a while you may start to see an image, hear words or intuit an emotion. You may see or feel something silly or simple, such as "a herd of sheep", or feel sad. Mention these images and feelings to your friend, but if you don't get a response, don't worry. Starting with people you know means you can learn to read the energies. Eventually you can tune into the objects of people you know nothing about.

Crystals

Around 4,000BCE, the Mesopotamians used the stars to predict the future. They also believed that crystals found in the earth were linked to the planets and the cosmos. The Ancient Greeks believed that every piece of clear quartz crystal was a fragment of the archetypal Crystal of Truth. Crystals are considered to be concentrated electromagnetic energy fields. Used as adornments throughout history, they help us access spiritual wisdom. As a divinatory tool, they can be cast onto a zodiac circle to harness the power of the planetary forces and to protect against negative energy. Or they can be laid out in a spread like the Tarot to provide answers to questions. You can also choose a crystal as your guide for the day ahead.

Blue lace agate on the Third Eye chakra promotes vision and clarity.

Stones for spiritual success

Aligning your own energy to a specific crystal, by wearing or carrying it for the day, means that you can draw on its associated qualities.

CRYSTAL	ATTRIBUTES	HOW TO USE
Clear quartz	A crystal of action.	Wear or carry this if you need to start afresh. Perfect for enhancing your psychic powers.
Opal	Enables you to see your own feelings clearly.	Wear or carry opal to feel more in tune with others.
Topaz	Great for expressing ideas, opening your mind and communicating.	Carry topaz to assist decision-making and for happy travelling.
Red agate	Helps you defend your rights, to prove a point. The stone of initiative.	Wear or carry red agate when you need a shot of courage.
Lapis lazuli	The "eye of wisdom". Promotes career path and gives life.	Carry or wear it when you want to discover deeper truths.
Onyx	For achieving goals, both material and spiritual.	Carry or wear onyx to determine what your true values are.
Blue lace agate	Promotes clarity and self-awareness.	Carry or wear blue lace agate when you want to drop old habits and move forward, or if you want a new vision for the future.
Tourmaline	Promotes harmony, tolerance and respect.	Wear or carry pink or green tourmaline when you are seeking new romance or a commitment.
Orange carnelian	Encourages progressive thinking and protects against envy.	Wear or carry this when you want to break free from conventional ideas or habits.

Crystals and the zodiac

This chart shows the 12 zodiac crystals, their keywords and their oracles. Wear the crystal associated with your sun sign to enhance intuitive powers. For self-empowerment, hold your crystal in one hand as you meditate on your

SIGN	CRYSTAL	KEYWORD	ORACLE
Aries	**Red carnelian**	Activate	Challenges ahead; someone is pushing their luck; you are driven to succeed.
Taurus	**Rose quartz**	Love	You are about to fall in love; all relationship problems can be resolved now; sensual pleasure is more important than ambition.
Gemini	**Citrine**	Communicate	Travel is favoured; you're making the right decision; focus on your goals for success.
Cancer	**Moonstone**	Belong	Trust in your intuition; your emotions are all over the place; someone in power may try to deceive you.

keyword for future success. For oracle work, fill a small pouch with 12 zodiac crystals. Remove a crystal with your eyes closed; the oracle reveals current issues and future outcomes.

SIGN	CRYSTAL	KEYWORD	ORACLE
Leo	Tiger's eye	Inspire	Dare to be different; dramatic and challenging love; don't let others tell you what to do.
Virgo	Peridot	Discriminate	Time to spread your wings; you need meaningful, serious relationships; discriminate with care.
Libra	Jade	Harmonize	Success in romance; you're in tune with universal energy so manifest your desires.
Scorpio	Malachite	Transform	Stay awake to opportunity; you can persuade yourself or others of anything; success in money and marriage.

Crystals and the zodiac (continued)

SIGN	CRYSTAL	KEYWORD	ORACLE
Sagittarius	**Turquoise**	Travel	Expand your repertoire of talents; love is boundless; a journey toward happiness.
Capricorn	**Obsidian**	Materialize	Don't give in to self-doubt; persevere in your ambitions; changes are indicated for the better.
Aquarius	**Amber**	Rationalize	Rationalize a situation; you or someone else is rebellious and radical; work with a vision.
Pisces	**Aquamarine**	Romance	The tide is turning in your favour; don't compromise for the sake of it; romance is in the air.

The crystal oracle

You can use crystals, like the Tarot, to help you access your psychic powers and use them as a beneficial healing aid (see page 122). When you have collected the 12 zodiac crystals, keep them safe in a pouch and use them as an oracle, either for a daily reading or for specific questions.

Questioning the crystals

Put your pouch of zodiac crystals and a piece of white quartz crystal (representing clarity and personal success) plus an amethyst (representing a shift in consciousness) on a table before you.

1 Sit quietly, relax and close your eyes. Focus on a question such as, "Is new romance coming my way?" Take one crystal from the pouch and place it in front of you. This is the Crystal of Light, representing your current energy and what you are putting out to the world.

2 Take another crystal. This is the Crystal of Shadows, representing people, outside influences or blockages.

3 The last crystal to choose is called the Crystal of Fortune, which represents the future outcome of your question.

4 Use the chart on pages 190–2 to help you interpret the crystals. For example, if you choose peridot as the Crystal of Light, tiger's eye as the Crystal of Shadows and citrine as the Crystal of Fortune, the answer to your question might be:

* You come across as very discriminating and cautious and seem serious about relationships.
* You are going to meet someone inspirational.
* If you really communicate and aren't shy this will turn out to be a fun-loving relationship.

Runes

Runes, like other divination tools, vibrate to a universal, or divine, energy. When you are using runes you are tapping into these vibrations and the universal power that will guide you to make important decisions. The runes will give you a fresh perspective on the current situation and tell you how you should act accordingly. They are objective and, like any oracle, they give great insight into yourself and your intentions, where you are going in life and what your personal journey is all about. The power of the runes helps you to tap into the depths of the cosmos for answers to all your questions.

Runic history

The word "rune" originates from a Gothic word, *runa,* which meant a "secret thing" or "mystery". The fortune-telling use of runes dates back several thousand years, when the runes were a magical system of symbols and glyphs carved into rocks. The earliest example found in Sweden dates to 1300BCE.

A Swedish standing stone covered in runes, warning passing strangers of the awesome power of the Norse gods.

Runes were first used by Germanic tribes, and were later adopted by the Vikings. The berserkers, fierce Norse warriors, would carve runes on their swords before going into battle, in the belief that nothing could then overcome their power. Runes were carved on standing stones and they were also used to mark ownership of personal items, such as boxes and combs. Runes were also used for magical

Look at each rune in turn – some you will feel drawn to, others not.

purposes. Many rune stones found in northern Europe have incantations, love spells or mysterious riddles to empower, protect or keep people away engraved on them. The Vikings believed that each rune tapped into the power of the Norse gods and that they were a gift from the chief god, Odin.

Methods for using runes

There are many different ways to cast runes (see overleaf); but it's a good idea to establish a personal ritual to help you concentrate and interpret outcomes. A single rune can also be taken randomly from the pouch to answer a question or you can lay out runes in spreads like those used for the Tarot (see pages 182–3). You can make your own runes by drawing runic scripts with an indelible marker on flat, smooth pebbles like these. You can find them either on a beach or in some New Age shops.

Casting the runes

Before you start, look at each rune in turn and observe your intuitive reaction to it. This will enable you to discover later whether your gut feelings were correct or not.

METHOD 1

1 Take a piece of plain cotton, silk or linen cloth (natural fibres are best for nurturing auspicious energy), measuring approximately 15 x 15in (40 x 40cm), and lay it out on a flat table. If you prefer to sit cross-legged in meditative pose, the floor is just as good.

2 Ask your question and concentrate.

3 Hold the pouch in one hand, shake it gently and then scatter all the runes onto the cloth. Ignore any that fall on the edge or beyond it.

4 Shut your eyes and gradually pass your fingers over the runes. Pick up any rune that "speaks" to you. If you are a beginner choose three runes, at most, and interpret them first (see pages 197–9). The more upright runes you have, the more

immediate the decision or action will be. If you have no upright runes, this simply means that any solution, however obvious, will be delayed for a while.

METHOD 2

1 Prepare in the same way as for Method 1. Ask your question and concentrate.

2 Without looking, remove five runes from the pouch; ones that seem to "speak" to you. Then scatter them onto the cloth. Ignore any that fall beyond it or just on its edge. Those that are left on the cloth are the ones to work with. Turn up any that have fallen symbol-side down.

3 Now interpret the runes in relation to your question.

Runes and their meanings

Each rune symbolizes a specific archetype or idea. These are the basic interpretations that are used today.

RUNE		KEYWORD	MEANING
WYRD		Destiny	Taking control of your own destiny. Making conscious decisions.
FEHU	ᚠ	Possessions	Prosperity and material fulfilment. What are your true values?
URUZ	ᚢ	Strength	You can overcome any obstacle. Embrace change and discover your potential.
THURISAZ	ᚦ	Challenge	Don't assume you know all the answers. Look before you leap.
ANSUZ	ᚨ	Messages	Communicate and you can pursue your dreams. Expect the unexpected – in the nicest sense.
RAIDHO	ᚱ	Journey	Travel is favoured, whether spiritual, mental or physical. Don't fear the unknown.
KENAZ	ᚲ	Clarity	Passion is important; your sexual and emotional happiness is at stake. Be honest.
GEBO	ᚷ	Relationship	Success in relationships. New romance; profitable business ventures are favoured.
WUNJO	ᚹ	Success	A lucky rune, favouring love, children, creativity, material gain – if you're willing to make an effort.
HAGALL	ᚺ	Delay	Challenges ahead, but these are stepping stones to achieving your goal.

Runes and their meanings (continued)

RUNE		KEYWORD	MEANING
NIED		Need	Change is necessary, you're clinging to the past, you're too needy. Give it up.
ISA		Standstill	You're in limbo or distant from someone. Open up. Defrost the emotional fridge.
JERA		Harvest	Reap the rewards of your efforts. Cultivate your confidence, nurture your skills.
EIHWAZ		Action	Decisive action is required; a chance to change your life.
PERTH		Secret	Time to reveal a secret or uncover a truth. A secret will be revealed to you.
ELHAZ		Self-control	A period of good fortune is coming your way. Love is favoured.
SIGEL		Vitality	Success and power. Rejuvenated in mind, body and spirit.
TIR		Competition	Fiery feelings, challenges, passion, career success.
BEORC		New beginnings	Time to let go of the past. Birth of romance, love, a new you, a child.
EHWAZ		Progress	All journeys are important; moving home, changing job, new plans – all favoured.
MANNAZ		Self-acceptance	Take responsibility for your actions and choices, but listen to objective advice.

Runes and their meanings (continued)

RUNE		KEYWORD	MEANING
LAGAZ		Intuition	A psychic friend has wonderful news, or you discover your psychic potential.
ING		Accomplishment	Success and feeling good about yourself are favoured. Milestone opportunity coming your way.
DAEG		Light	Make a new start; turn your dreams into reality.
OTHEL		Possession	Financial benefits, but your love values are in question. Focus on what you want, but more importantly why.

Keep your runes safe in a cloth pouch. You can draw one out first thing in the morning to see what kind of day you can expect.

I Ching

Derived from an ancient Chinese system of divining the future from the patterns in nature, such as the lines on a tortoise's shell, the I Ching dates back thousands of years. The I Ching, or "Book of Changes" is based on the symbolism of yin and yang, the origins of which are shrouded in mystery. These two opposing energies are represented in the I Ching's eight trigrams or groups of three lines (see page 203), symbolizing all that happens, moves or changes in life. Pairing up the trigrams creates 64 hexagrams (groups of six lines), which represent 64 different oracles.

   The discovery of the I Ching is attributed to the legendary first Emperor of China, Fu Hsi, who believed that nature's basic patterns reveal everything we do. He created the eight "trigrams" that form the basis of the I Ching, representing the eight fundamental energies of nature. In the 6th century BCE, the well-known philosopher and sage Confucius developed the I Ching to become an integral part of Chinese culture. In the 19th century Richard Wilhelm, a German missionary, translated the texts. Not long after, the psychologist Carl Jung saw the I Ching as a confirmation of his own theories about synchronicity. He believed that meaningful coincidences take on greater significance when more than one occurs simultaneously, such as happens with the throwing of the coins in the I Ching, when the question being asked and the pattern formed a hexagram. It is beyond the scope of this book to give interpretations for all 64 I Ching oracles, so to get started, you will just learn to use the eight basic oracles. As a divination tool, similar to the runes and the Tarot, the random throwing of coins (see page 202) puts you in touch with the universal energy and its wisdom. Work with the eight trigrams before progressing to the hexagrams, to get a sense of how to use the I Ching and discover whether it feels right for you or not.

Yin and yang

Yin is associated with all things "feminine" such as the moon, silence, darkness, psychic and intuitive power, the winter, feelings and the right brain. Yang is associated with all things "masculine" such as the sun, the summer, heat, noise, light, intellectual and rationalizing power and the left brain.

The symbol for yang is a single unbroken line and the symbol for yin is a single broken line:

The eight trigrams are each made up of three yin and yang lines in various combinations (see page 203). These are the building blocks of the system, representing the eight natural energies in the universe: heaven, earth, thunder, water, mountain, wind/wood, fire and lake. Work with the fundamental energies as shown on the following pages.

Bamboo sticks used for divination at Wong Tai Sin temple, Hong Kong.

The yin-yang symbol shown on an antique Chinese compass used for feng shui.

Coin consultation

1 Choose three coins of the same size, with distinct heads and tails.

2 When you are ready, take the coins and shake them gently in your cupped hands while you think of a simple question.

3 Throw the coins three times (if you are using all the hexagrams, throw the coins six times). Each throw represents one line of a trigram or a hexagram, starting from the bottom.

4 Write down the result for each line. Give value to each side of the coin as follows: heads = 3, tails = 2.

Your first throw represents the bottom line; the second throw the middle line and the third throw the top line. A total score of 6, 7, 8 or 9 can be obtained in each throw, giving you either a yin line (broken line) or a yang line (unbroken line). 6 and 8 are yin lines; 7 and 9 are yang lines.

For example, say you threw:

* First throw (bottom line) – 2 tails and 1 head = 7
* Second throw (middle line) 3 heads = 9
* Third throw (top line) 2 heads and one tail = 8

You would write down in ascending order: 7, 9, 8. In other words, at the bottom a yang line, in the middle a yang line and at the top a yin line. Your trigram would look like this: ☶

Now look at the interpretations for the different trigrams for your answer (see chart right). The interpretations for the complete set of 64 hexagrams (see pages 204–7) can also be used either by increasing your number of throws to six, to create six lines in ascending order, or simply as an "open oracle". Close your eyes, flick through the relevant pages in the book and then stop when you feel ready and move your finger over the page. Whenever your finger stops, open your eyes to read the oracle.

The eight trigrams

The eight trigrams represent some deeply held philosophical Taoist concepts. Here, keywords are based on the original ideas, but the meanings are modern interpretations to work with your own intuition.

TRIGRAM	KEYWORD	MEANING
CH'IEN heaven	The creative	Time to aim high, unleash your potential, be confident.
K'UN earth	The receptive	Acceptance and patience are needed now; things will happen in good time.
CHEN thunder	The arousing	Awakening to new ideas, sudden insights; a flash of inspiration brings success.
K'AN water	The abysmal	Trust your feelings and instincts; don't resist the energy, go with the flow.
KEN mountain	Keeping still	Spiritual work is beneficial; take time to reflect on your feelings; there is a need for stillness.
SUN wind/wood	The gentle	Be fair with yourself, don't let others push you around. Soon you will succeed.
LI fire	The clinging	Passion, love and closeness are favoured. Clear your mind, let go of the past, move on.
TUI lake	The joyous	Within you are all the secrets of the universe; get in touch with your own magic.

The 64 hexagrams

HEXAGRAM		KEYWORD	MEANING
1 CH'IEN		The creative	Take control of your life and make a decision now.
2 K'UN		The receptive	Listen to advice from someone with experience.
3 CHUN		Difficulties	Rivals abound; go with your instinct on who to trust.
4 MENG		Immaturity	Don't get carried away by an impossible dream.
5 HSU		Waiting	Remain calm and everything will work out well.
6 SUNG		Conflict	Communicate your thoughts to avoid conflict.
7 SHIH		The army	Be a leader for others and you'll achieve success.
8 PI		Holding together	Give someone their space and gain your own, too.
9 HSAIO CH'U		Taming by the small	What you do now will reap rewards tomorrow.
10 LU		Conduct	Someone can now accept you for who you are.
11 TAI		Peace	Anything you start now will reap rewards.
12 P'I		Standstill	Feeling stuck lets you modify your plans.
13 T'UNG JEN		Fellowship	Compromise to bring good results.
14 TA YU		Possessing plenty	You are about to enter a phase of abundance.
15 CH'IEN		Modesty	Be serene and others will see your real talents.
16 YU		Enthusiasm	You will be given a new opportunity.

HEXAGRAM		KEYWORD	MEANING
17 SU		Following	Welcome change rather than fear it.
18 KU		Removing corruption	Self-repair needed to show strength of character.
19 LIN		Approach	Unexpected opportunities lighten your pathway.
20 KUAN		Contemplation	Reflect carefully on any decision facing you.
21 SHIH HO		Biting through	Be frank about what you truly want.
22 PI		Grace	Be sincere and let your beauty shine through.
23 PO		Splitting apart	Things fall apart to fall together again.
24 FU		Return	You are on the threshold of an exciting new era.
25 WU WANG		Innocence	The future will unfold in the way you want.
26 TA CH'U		Taming by the great	Stay calm and all will be resolved.
27 I		The open mouth	Self-discipline will bring you happiness.
28 TA KUO		Preponderance of the great	You can never escape yourself.
29 K'AN		The abysmal	Go with the flow of your feelings.
30 LI		The clinging	Someone will adore your inner fire.
31 HSIEN		Influence	Welcome a new love affair or even marriage.
32 HENG		Duration	Good fortune will come from integrity.

The 64 hexagrams (continued)

HEXAGRAM		KEYWORD	MEANING
33 TUN		Retreat	Take a break and think carefully.
34 TA CHUANG		Power of the great	Be emotionally honest with yourself.
35 CHIN		Progress	Whatever you want can now be realized.
36 MING I		Darkening of the light	Re-evaluate your plans and leave the situation.
37 CHI JEN		The family	Loyalty needed now to improve relationships.
38 K'UEI		Opposition	Misunderstandings abound; take care.
39 CHIEN		Obstruction	The blockage is all in your mind.
40 HSIEH		Deliverance	It's time to forgive and forget.
41 SUN		Decrease	Don't underestimate your goals.
42 I		Increase	Be creative with your ideas and gain influence.
43 KUAI		Breakthrough	The turning point has arrived.
44 KOU		Coming to meet	Temptation by someone or something: be careful!
45 TS'UI		Gathering together	Get together with those you can trust.
46 SHENG		Pushing upward	*How* a goal is won is more important than the goal.
47 K'UN		Oppression	Testing times, so believe in yourself.
48 CHING		The well	Plumb the depths of your wisdom for results.

HEXAGRAM		KEYWORD	MEANING
49 KO		Revolution	Change is needed in some aspect of your life.
50 TING		The cauldron	Nurture your dreams and make them real.
51 CHEN		The arousing	Unpredictable events are exciting.
52 KEN		Keeping still	Don't let someone distract you from your goal.
53 CHIEN		Development	Lower your expectations and you'll succeed.
54 KUEI MEI		Marrying maiden	Romance is coming from an unexpected direction.
55 FENG		Abundance	Move on from the past and live for the moment.
56 LU		The wanderer	It's time to go on a special journey.
57 SUN		The gentle	Be firm about your intentions to someone.
58 TUI		The joyous	Fulfilling relationships around the corner.
59 HUAN		Dispersion	Sacrifice a short-term goal for a long-term benefit.
60 CHIEH		Limitation	Start saying "No" when you mean it.
61 CHUNG FU		Inner truth	Follow the path that has heart for you.
62 HSIAO KUO		Preponderance of the small	Wait for the air to clear and don't take a risk.
63 CHI CHI		After completion	Work at a relationship problem – don't ignore it.
64 WEI CHI		Before completion	Prepare yourself for the great things to come.

Automatic writing

Also known as "psychography", automatic writing is a simple and effective way to channel information from the universal storehouse of all knowledge. This divination aid is often used by mediums and channellers to contact spirit guides. However, it is not necessary to rely on a spirit guide for information, as this can be channelled solely by the Higher Self in contact with the cosmos. Automatic writing can access all the ideas, knowledge and wisdom that is, has been and ever will be known. It involves deliberately altering your state of consciousness using the methods explained throughout this book.

First try another exercise in right-brain work: mirror-writing (see page 210).

Irish medium and author of more than 20 books, Geraldine Cummins specialized in automatic writing or psychography, which she called "transmitted writing". She claimed to exercise no control or censorship over her results.

The purpose of this exercise is to learn how to divert your mind from logical right-brain writing to the mysterious world of writing as though you were reflecting your writing in a mirror. If you are left-handed, you may be able to do it without thinking. Mirror-writing will become as natural to you as walking. If you are right-handed, it may prove to be more challenging.

According to scientific research, the ability to write "back to front" or do mirror-writing is a genetic trait. Only about one in 6,500 people can do it without interrupting the flow of joined-up writing. Leonardo da Vinci used mirror-writing as a form of code, so that no one else could read his work. Practising mirror-writing will free you from the conscious investment of left-brain writing and prepare yourself for "right-brain", automatic writing.

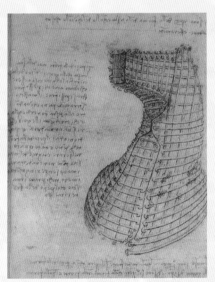

An example of a working drawing of an iron hook by left-handed Leonardo da Vinci (1452–1590). He has used mirror-writing, to the left of the sketch, to serve as code.

Practising mirror-writing and intuitive writing

Sometimes we need to push our right brain into gear, rather than just let it work of its own accord. This exercise may feel uncomfortable if you are naturally right-handed, or very left-brain oriented. But it will do your psychic powers a world of good.

1 First, write your name in big letters on a piece of paper. Hold it in front of a mirror. What do you see? Does it resemble your name? Does it look mysterious, different or vaguely familiar? It is still your name, but it won't resemble your name or your writing.

2 Now sit somewhere quiet and take up your pen and paper. This time you are going to write your name backward, from the right-hand side to the left-hand side of the page, as mirror-writing. This can feel quite challenging as it forces you to think from your right brain. If you can only manage one letter at a time, even uppercase and unjoined, it doesn't matter.

If you can, join up your writing and let it flow freely; you may even find that you can do your automatic writing like this. Some people find processing the reversal of the image easier than others; left-handed people usually have an advantage.

3 Next, try some right-brain, intuitive writing. Take your pen, begin to write normally from left to right, then turn your attention away to read a book, make a phone call or watch television. Let your hand continue to write, but don't be conscious of what you are writing. Look at what you have written after a couple of minutes.

The next level: automatic writing

This sense-inspired psychic tool combines your personal handwriting, like a fingerprint unique to you, with your psychic powers. With practice, it enhances your imagination and right-brain power.

1 Think of a question.

2 Then relax, go to your psychic sanctuary (see page 100–1) and protect yourself in your bubble of light (see page 61). Repeat aloud three times, "What I write will come to me via my Higher Self, directly from the sea of unconscious knowledge." This will also prevent any negative spirits from contaminating the information or interfering in your channelling, while you are still a beginner in psychic work.

3 Now, in your calm, peaceful state, eyes closed, place your pen on the paper and let your hand start to write. Words, sentences or whole paragraphs may appear, but sometimes you will see symbols or doodle-like squiggles. Often, your writing will be illegible, without proper grammar or punctuation. After about five minutes, you can count yourself out of your state, "One, two, three and I shall be awake."

4 Then look at what you have written. If there is an answer to your question it may be relayed in a very symbolic way – but you will know what it means.

Automatic writing with spirit guides

If you would like to contact a spirit guide, then read Chapter Seven (see pages 236–271) before using automatic writing. These messages can be written in other languages and signed by unknown entities. The messages can also reveal secrets or send information you may not have requested or which you find offensive. If the energies feel uncomfortable, then you must know how to deal with them (see page 246). But if you feel happy about your guide, then ask who they are and why they are writing through you.

chapter 6

Altered states

Although most psychic work is undertaken in a basic
altered state of consciousness – meditational yet
embracing an awareness of the Higher Self – there are
other altered states that require deeper work and the
willingness to go beyond normal boundaries. We may be
sceptical about these changes of consciousness, but going
beyond the known states of hypnosis, which still admits to
an alerted sense of awareness, into conditions in which we
can leave the body, experience astral travel or enter the
realms of the unconscious and come back to tell the tale, is
considered today to be possible – though unproven. In this
chapter, we look at how close to the edge of the universe
you can get, if you truly want to.

Shamanism

Shamanism is the practice of communicating and interacting with the supernatural world. It is thought to be the earliest form of spiritual practice, dating back thousands of years to when most peoples were animists, believing that every animal, tree, rock or landscape on earth and in heaven was imbued with spirit. The world was alive with animated energy flowing through all things, including man himself.

Role of the shaman

The word "shaman" means "he or she who knows". The spiritual healers of indigenous groups, shamans usually worked alone. Having undergone initiation or ritualistic transformation, they entered a deep trance to enable them to leave the body and journey to an animated, supernatural world, where they would meet spirit guides, power animals or spirit masters, to invoke revelations and return to "reality" to heal others.

Marks of spiritual power

Shamans have specific symbols, totems, rituals and codes to separate them from the rest of the community. These include dance, taboos, amulets, talismans and symbolic codes displayed on clothing or on the skin in tattoo form. For shamans, the plants and even rocks and landscapes have their own spirits and healing powers. The rite of passage to becoming a shaman is usually through a form of psychological or induced crisis, according to mythologist Joseph Campbell. For example, the Peruvian Urarina use a ritualistic tea made with the hallucinogenic plant substance ayahuasca to induce shamanic power. Many Native Americans believe an initiate must go out into the wilderness to experience a spiritual awakening by meeting a spirit guide on a special quest.

Items being used as part of a shamanic ceremony in Bolivia.

Shamanic practice wordwide

Some shamans, such as the South American Tapirape, are "called" in their dreams. Other means of entering the shamanic trance-like state include drumming, consuming psychedelic mushrooms, spending time in sweat lodges and engaging in dance to induce trance. Shamans can still be found among the Uralic peoples of Russia and Sibera and, in Asia, in small communities in Tibet, Nepal, Vietnam and Taiwan. In South America, the Curanderos and Ayahuasqueros are practising folk-healers and shamans, while there are also shamans among the Inuits of North America and Canada, as well as in Africa, Papua New Guinea and Australia.

Modern shamanism

What is termed "core shamanism" has recently made a comeback, thanks to the work of American anthropologist Michael Harner. After establishing the Foundation for Shamanic Studies in 1984, Harner's universal shamanism has become widely popularized in the West. He believes that the point of shamanism is that each of us can discover another reality and through that realize that we are not separate from one another, or from the universe. To access the spiritual realms, Harner has developed shamanic workshops and study courses available to everyone, believing that these teachings make union with the entire cosmos possible.

Many nomadic peoples of Sibera, Mongolia and China still perform rituals and festivals to celebrate their shamanic heritage and traditions. Not far from the Mongolian border, at the Kundustug Springs, an ethno-cultural festival known as Khoomei takes place annually and Tuvan shamans still perform the ancient trance ritual known as Kamlanie (pictured).

Two realities

Depending on one's state of consciousness, we are able to perceive two realities. First, there is what Harner calls the "ordinary state of consciousness" (OSC), where one perceives "ordinary reality" (OR). Those in the "shamanic state of consciousness" (SSC) are able to enter into and perceive "non-ordinary reality" (NOR). Both are classified as "realities" because they are both subjective encounters.

Each state is recognized as having its own forms of knowledge and relevance to human existence. Shamanic practitioners must learn to alter their state of consciousness to perceive successfully what others do not, and gain the ability to move back and forth at will between these realities in order to heal and help others. Spirits encountered in NOR are considered real by shamanic practitioners because they interact with them at first hand. This interaction involves direct perception with all the senses. In NOR, shamanic practitioners routinely see, touch, smell and hear spirits, some of which become personal helpers or guides, who often provide miraculous help in healing and divination.

Contemporary practice

Simon Buxton, founder of the Sacred Trust and the UK Faculty for the Foundation for Shamanic Studies, runs the foremost core shamanic training organization in the world in myth and dreamwork. Workshops include visionary exploration of the classic shamanic journey. Initiation into the shamanic state is assisted by drumming and movement techniques.

Most of modern shamanic practice is to solve problems and work with nature to restore the balance and harmony of the earth and the universe. This involves cultivating a deep respect for the planet and its inhabitants at a spiritual level. There are also techniques for spiritual healing as well as darkness workshops, where participants journey to encounter the cosmic sea of energy.

Accessing the world of the shaman

This technique will give you an understanding of the invisible world of the shaman. Being, or imagining yourself to be, invisible means you can access other realities in safety. Wearing a "cloak of invisibility", you can move between the spiritual world and the material world without being seen by other entities. However, it does not entitle you to cheat, steal or get away with negative actions in either world. All shamanic work must be done for the good of all in the universe. Try it only if you have already worked with all the visualization and meditation techniques described in this book so far.

1 Sit somewhere quiet and comfortable. Relax into your psychic sanctuary (see pages 100–1). Visualize the canopy of the stars above you on a dark night. As you see the constellations and the infinite darkness, imagine that the sky is a huge dark cloak studded with stars. It is the cloak of the Goddess of the Night, Nyx, whose home lies on the far edge of the cosmos.

2 Now let Nyx's cloak of darkness, velvet and silk, black and enveloping, wrap itself around you, until you are within her darkness. Now let the light of this darkness fill every pore of your skin, from your head down to your toes. Let the darkness stay with you for a while and realize that you are now invisible. Stay awhile in your invisibility, imagining that if you were to walk down a street, no one would see you.

3 To return to the world of visibility, gradually imagine that you are taking off the cloak of the night. Let it fall all around you, as the Goddess of the Day, Hemera, reaches out her arms to welcome you back. Take a deep breath and gradually come back into the daytime of your ordinary reality.

Hypnosis

"Hypnosis" comes from the Greek word *hypnos,* meaning sleep. The state of hypnosis is very similar to the trance-inducing techniques of meditation, where the individual is in a calm, relaxed, but alert, state of focused attention.

The history of hypnosis

In 1843, the Scottish neurosurgeon, James Braid, coined the term "neuro-hypnotism" (sleep of the nervous system). He had previously studied mesmerism after seeing the French mesmerist Charles Lafontaine perform and realizing that the subjects were in a different state from both normal consciousness and real sleep.

Braid's work subsequently influenced a French country doctor, Ambroise-Auguste Liébeault, who was later acknowledged as the founder of hypnotherapy. Visitors to Liébault's School of Hypnotherapy in Nancy, France, included Sigmund Freud and Émile Coué, a notable psychologist who introduced a self-improvement therapy called "optimistic autosuggestion", which was popular in the 1920s. Braid's opinion of mesmerism (often confused with hypnotism) was that Mesmer's occult animal magnetism was an illusion and its influence on the subject merely verbal suggestion.

Mainstream therapy

Since the 1920s, hypnosis has become part of mainstream psychotherapy. In 2001 the British Psychological Society (BPA) reported that "hypnosis is a valid subject for scientific study and research and a proven therapeutic medium."

James Randi, a professional magician and sceptic, sees the process of hypnosis as a kind of conscious collusion between the hypnotist and the client in that, whatever the hypnotist suggests, the client cooperates or obliges. In 2005 the American Psychological Association (APA) made its own findings known. It stated that the client is guided to respond to the subjective changes that are suggested by the hypnotist. This creates an improved alteration in the sensations, emotion, perception and behaviour of the subject. The APA also believed that self-hypnosis was a viable method for changing one's own behaviour.

Émile Coué introduced a self-improvement therapy that included a mantra-like auto-suggestion that continues to be well known today: "Every day, in every way, I'm getting better and better."

Self-hypnosis

The technique of self-hypnosis is currently used to help reduce stress, make helpful lifestyle changes, give up old destructive habits and deal with psychological problems, such as anxiety, depression and low self-esteem. The technique is also useful as a means of entering into deeper psychic realm to get in touch with your Higher Self, or spirit guides, or for cosmic ordering.

It is through our personal unconscious that we can know our truths and delve further into the collective unconscious, too. Self-hypnosis allows you to look into the mirror of the Self, without emotional investment.

Using self-hypnosis

Self-hypnosis is a mixture of meditation, visualization and self-affirmation. Using the "lighthouse" sanctuary idea (see pages 100–1), this exercise will help you develop all your powers of psychic insight. This form of self-hypnosis can be used to get rid of bad habits, too – such as visualizing putting your chocolate obsession into a bottle and sending it away!

1 Relax in a place of tranquillity. Imagine each part of your body closing down, releasing tension, opening up to the relaxation techniques that you have already learned in this book.

2 Close your eyes and count down from 20 slowly or in time with each out-breath. Imagine you are walking down the steps from the door of the lighthouse sanctuary. You are descending the steps toward the sea. With each step, the light from the lighthouse gradually dims, until you arrive on a beach in darkness. Here there is only the gently whooshing of the sea as it laps on the shore edge.

3 Now, as you listen to the whoosh of the surf, each time you hear the sound "whoosh", make an affirmation or good intention. Then place those intentions in a bottle and throw it into the sea. The intention may be in the form of a letter or words, a sound or a visual image of what you want. But whatever it is, you are now placing it in the care of the universe. Then ask for a reply, to acknowledge that the message in a bottle has been safely received.

4 Thank the cosmos and then close down the self-hypnosis slowly, by counting back up to 20 as you go back up the steps to your lighthouse door. You have now asked the cosmos to bless your future intentions.

Out-of-body experiences

Radio executive Robert Allan Monroe became known for his research into altered states of consciousness. His 1971 book *Journeys Out of the Body* is credited with popularizing the term "out-of-body experience" (OBE). A pioneer in the exploration of human consciousness, he set up the Monroe Institute in the US; a "gateway" programme of training, which allows students to reach altered states of higher consciousness via meditation, visualization and other techniques.

OBEs: an explanation

The out-of-body experience is a sensation that you are outside your body and, in many cases, literally able to view your physical body from another place, even miles above the earth. OBEs are usually spontaneous, but they can be induced. The simplest explanation of OBEs is that the human consciousness separates from the human body and travels unhindered by any physical form through the physical world. People who have experienced OBEs claim that they actually willed themselves out of their bodies, or were dragged out by some unknown force or had a spontaneous realization that they were not inhabiting their bodies.

The dream state

OBEs usually occur when the person is on the verge of sleep, or entering or leaving REM sleep or in a lucid dream state. Many people have argued that the OBE is actually some kind of dream. However, an ordinary dream does not have the important features of the subject seeming to leave the body and being conscious of perceiving things from outside the self or the ability to view oneself from another place.

A bird's eye view of one of the Nazca lines. It has been suggested that these giant drawings are the size they are because they are shamanic visions from an out-of-body experience.

Induced OBEs

There are many different ways of consciously entering into an OBE state, including the forearm trick devised by OBE pioneer Sylvan Muldoon. To try this for yourself, hold your forearm perpendicularly above yourself in bed as you drift off to sleep; your arm will drop down, restoring your mind. This deliberate attempt to remain on the edge between wakefulness and sleep induces a trance-like effect, which can help to set off the sensation of OBE.

Psychologists and scientists have done extensive research into other mechanical inductions of OBEs. These include magnetic stimulation of the brain, sensory deprivation, sensory overload and brainwave synchronization. OBEs can also be induced through hallucinogenic drugs.

Other methods of inducing OBEs include lucid dreaming practice and deep-trance and visualization work, including imagining a cord or rope literally pulling one's self out of one's body, sensations of floating or imagining the projection of one's mind into the air.

Research into OBEs

Neurological explanations suggest that OBEs are simply the stimulation of various parts of the brain. Susan Blackmore, an English psychologist, believes that the person loses contact with the sensory input from the body. The world that the individual views is not generated by sensory information but by the brain's ability to create replicas of the physical world, as it does every night in our dreams.

Olaf Blanke in Switzerland, neuroscientist Michael Persinger in the US and, more recently, Henrik Ehrsson in the UK, have all conducted studies and experiments to prove that there are normal neurological reasons why individuals experience OBEs. Neurologists believe the experience is triggered by a discrepancy between visual and tactile signals. However, this doesn't explain why people can describe people, events or places a distance away from their own physical presence.

One technique that you can try is the popular Golden Dawn Body of Light Technique (see page 228–9). The Golden Dawn was an occult society active in the UK during the late 19th and early 20th centuries. Concerned with the practice of magic and spiritual development, it has been a major influence on occult arts in the West ever since.

Through our imagination we enter previously unknown worlds. By merging imagination with an altered state of awareness, many people have sensed that they are no longer confined within their physical body.

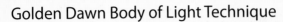

Golden Dawn Body of Light Technique

Use your imagination to travel out of your physical body, into the psychic realm. Do this exercise every day for about a week, spending about 5–10 minutes on it each time, until you find you can easily "see yourself" across the room. This technique is challenging and it is very difficult to describe, but you will know it when you have moved your mind into the other image of yourself. As a mirror image of you, this image can go anywhere you want it to go. You can walk through walls, across oceans, around the world or even out into the cosmos.

Once you are able to project yourself into this image, you can project this new "you" anywhere and experience this other sense of your self. You may often feel as if a part of you is out of your body. This is one way to experience astral travel.

1 Begin by finding a comfortable chair in a room where you will not be disturbed. Then relax, using any method you find that works for you. Keep your eyes open or closed, depending on which is easier.

2 Now visualize yourself standing across the room from where you are sitting, as if you were looking in a mirror. Try to "see" yourself in detail. See the colour of your eyes, the colours and details of your clothes, jewelry and accessories, your skin, your hair and the expression on your face. Get to know your appearance, but without making any judgment. Alternatively, you can imagine yourself in a completely different guise, if you find that easier. Take the time to build up your imaginary figure of yourself.

You, too, can project a part of yourself out into the "real" world and experience the liberation of astral travel.

3 Next practise imagining walking around in certain places you know. Imagine walking into work or to the local café, the shopping mall, your home or your friend's house. Visualize yourself in all these places and start to get a sense of the details of your experiences there. What does each place smell of? Who's there? Is it busy? Is it noisy or quiet? Once you feel comfortable with this imagery, move on to the next stage.

4 Now, instead of seeing yourself as a mirror image, you "become" the mirror image. Project your mind into the image you have created outside of yourself. This is called your "body of light". Imagine you are looking out through the eyes of the body of light of your new self.

Astral travel

Associated with OBEs, astral travel is concerned with the existence of the astral body, a subtle body separate from the physical one, capable of travelling outside it in the astral plane. Astral travelling is an intentional act rather than a spontaneous one and there are two pathways. One is traditionally known simply as "astral travel", through which, from a projected sense of self, we experience everything physical, including the physical, original self. This is the experience that led Robert Monroe to coin the phrase "out-of-body experience". The second pathway is known as astral projection, through which the spiritual body, also known as the astral or etheric body

(see page 32), is capable of travelling outside the physical body to non-physical realms.

These realms, or planes, are also called astral, etheric or spiritual. The experience is described as that of the soul, leaving both the physical body and the physical world to travel to other dimensions, often with no sense of time or place. The astral world has been known as the "world of illusion" or "world of thoughts".

Astral travel can take us beyond our perception of the limits of space and time. It is an awareness of infinity and the "eternal now". Whatever you meet, see or discover is a unique personal experience.

Historical perspective

According to Classical and Renaissance Neoplatonists, the astral body is an intermediate body of light linking soul to physical body, while the astral plane is an intermediate world of light between heaven and earth, comprising the spheres of the planets and stars. These astral spheres were held to be populated by angels, demons and spirits. The 3rd-century philosopher Plotinus believed "the rational soul ... is akin to the great Soul of the World" while "the material universe, like the body, is made as a faded image of the Intelligible". These bodies and their planes of being are depicted as concentric circles or nested spheres, with a separate body traversing each realm.

Soul travel

The idea of the astral body figured prominently in the work of the 19th-century French occultist Eliphas Lévi and was adopted by the Theosophists and the Golden Dawn. "Soul travel" appears in various other religious traditions; for example, Ancient Egyptian teachings taught that the soul, known as the *ka*, hovered outside the physical body to reunite with the *ba*, or spirit, at physical death. In Japanese mythology, *ikiryō* is a manifestation of the soul of a living person, existing separately from the body, protecting the individual from negative energy. The belief that when one sleeps the soul leaves the body and seeks lessons in other planes is key to the religion of Eckankar, founded in 1965, focusing on spiritual exercises enabling practitioners to experience the "Light and Sound of God".

The expression "astral projection" is still used in two different ways. For the followers of the Golden Dawn and some Theosophists it retained the classical meaning of journeying to other worlds, the astrological spheres and other imaginery landscapes, but outside these circles the term was increasingly applied to non-physical travel.

The Ancient Egyptian portrayal of the *ka*, a spiritual double that resides in each man. This representation has two upraised arms on the head, reaching for the sky, which is the sign for the word *ka* in the Egyptian language.

Near-death experiences

One of the earliest recorded "near-death experiences" (or NDEs) was in the myth of Er from Plato's *Republic* (*c*. 380BCE); a story of a man who returned from the dead to recount his experience of the spiritual world. More recently, American John C. Wheeler was certified dead after a drowning accident, only to revive the next day. In his published account he records his experience of a spiritual state of existence.

Common experiences

Most subjects report having these experiences during major surgery and traumatic events such as car accidents, near-drownings and heart attacks. People who have claimed to have near-death experiences often talk of the feeling that they still have a "body", but of a very different nature to the one they left behind. Commonly, they glimpse the spirits of relatives and friends who have already died and approach some sort of barrier or border, representing the limit between earthly life and the spirit world. They are usually overwhelmed by intense feelings of joy, love and peace. Despite this, they reunite with their physical body and live.

Scientific research

With considerable debate in scientific circles, research continues to be carried out on near-death experiences in hospitals worldwide. Medical researcher and author of *What Happens When We Die,* Sam Parnia, concluded there was as yet no evidence of what NDEs actually are. Meanwhile, British neurophysicist Dr Peter Fenwick who examined over 300 NDE cases, concluded that the mind and brain appeared to be actually separate, posing an enormous problem for the scientific community.

Characteristics of NDEs

Near-death experiences tend to include many of the following features:

* Physically the body is literally dead, in a coma or deeply unconscious.

* There is no premeditation involved and the body is not under the control of the individual.

* The individual sees spirits, hears music and perhaps meets an angel or some other heavenly figure.

* There is a deep feeling of eternal peace and connected oneness.

* The individual passes through or approaches a channel of bright light.

* The soul reviews the individual's life.

* The individual is offered a chance to return to the body or is told to return to it.

The belief that one has experienced death, or been very close to death and seen beyond the limits of life, has fascinated people for centuries. Currently, scientists are trying to find out whether near-death experiences really are possible or "all in the mind".

chapter 7

Other dimensions

Exploring other dimensions of the supernatural world
expands your mind and imagination and enables you
to develop your psychic powers even further. This chapter
is a guide to the outer reaches of the spiritual world, from
contacting spirit guides and ascended masters to
channelling and experiencing past lives. Mediums act as
filters, or conduits, for messages between the spiritual and
mundane worlds, while spiritual questing and
communicating with guardian angels are also ways to
utilize our psychic powers. By raising our consciousness to
align with our Higher Self, we can contact other planes of
existence, including the mysterious, yet controversial,
world of ghosts that holds a fascination for many.

Spirit guides and ascended masters

At some point in our lives, we have probably all felt that someone is "watching over" us or that we have some kind of spiritual guide, friend, angel or special animal friend who helps us get through difficult times, pointing us to the right pathway when we have to make choices. Calling on these spirit guides requires a particular ability to use your right-brain altered state of consciousness, coupled with an awareness of being truly grounded in the tangible world.

Most important for this kind of work is to take responsibility for what you are doing, to thank the spirits for their guidance, close down your chakras (see page 102) and return to the "ordinary" world when you have finished speaking with your guide, in order to protect yourself from any unwanted negative energy.

A word of warning

As with any psychic work, if you are truly looking for good guides, it is the "good guys" who will come to you. If at any time you feel you are under negative influences, do not continue with this work. Please read pages 88–93 on psychic protection before undergoing any work with spirits and also use the special protective ritual on the facing page.

Spirit guides can appear in many different guises, both as symbolic imagery in our everyday world, or as a visual, oral or other intuitive or imaginative experiences. These guises give us a sense of their presence in the psychic realms. Reaching out into the spiritual world to ask for help from your guides is simply a question of going first into your psychic sanctuary (see pages 100–1) and performing a simple ritual to protect and empower you and to reinforce your spirit guide's assistance.

Protection ritual

This ritual is a further development of the exercise on page 61 (How to create a psychic protection field). You can use both exercises as a double boost of protection when you are entering unknown psychic territory.

Go to your psychic sanctuary as described on pages 100–1. This time imagine that a golden light of peace, calm and harmony flows through you. It enters via your Crown Chakra, then slowly permeates your whole body, filling every pore and emanating throughout all your chakras, your aura and subtle body energies, until you are surrounded and infused by a golden light of protection. Now you can continue to find your spirit guide.

Angels in the Christian tradition have long been thought of as protective spirit guides. This illustration is called *Angels Casting Stars Through the Sky Like Seed* by Edward Burne-Jones, from *The Flower Book* (1905).

Power animals

In many indigenous tribes, animal totems and spirit guides were used to help and protect shamans and priests during their spiritual journeys. Calling on a power animal creates a natural, empowering energy. Choosing your animal often symbolizes your own desires, character and life journey.

Power animals and their meanings

This selection of animals represents some of the energies that you might be hoping to bring into your life, such as courage, wisdom or love. If you harness these animals' powers, they will protect and boost your own energy levels to achieve what you truly want, or teach you what you need to know.

Animal	Meaning
Ram	Achievement, success
Hare	Psychic power, renewal
Owl	Wisdom
Stag	Independence
Deer	Romance
Fox	Diplomacy
Wolf	Learning, life paths
Dog	Protection, kinship
Hawk	Pride, far-sightedness
Horse	Freedom, movement
Snake	Healing, transformation
Bull	Wealth, creativity

Spirit or teacher guides

Many spirit guides represent archetypal or symbolic qualities that may need expression in your life, which may be why they come into your world as people. You may find that your spirit guide is an artist, a wise woman, a warrior, a teacher, a healer, a monk or a musician. Usually the guide has come to you to show you a pathway that you need to follow, or to guide you in a certain way that is appropriate to your current life situation. They may also give you answers to specific questions and then move on. Another guide will then come along to help in a different way. Their insight or answers can come to you through dreams or in meditation.

Meeting your power animal

To help you know your personal power animal, follow this simple visualization technique.

1 Perform the protection rituals described on pages 61 and 239. Close your eyes and relax.

2 Imagine you are in a forest glade with tall trees all around and you feel at one with nature. You are in your Golden Light, knowing that no one can harm you, nothing can disturb you and you are safe.

3 Sit on a grassy bank and see another warm Golden Light in the distance, between the trees. You know that this is a friend; you have met your power animal before in some other life or in some other place. Now you wait for your animal to come to you. Call gently in your imagination, as if calling to an animal to come to you. As the Golden Light moves closer, you see the animal that has chosen to guide you. In your mind ask their name or what they can help you with.

4 Once you have discovered what you wanted to know, or just felt the presence of a comforting guide, thank the animal and come back to normal consciousness.

5 Close down your chakras by imagining that each one is a flower closing up for the night (see page 102) and then stamp your feet twice on the floor as a sign that you have finished the session. You can call on your animal to help you at any time. You can also carry a symbol of that animal to take with you wherever you go.

Ascended masters, or spiritual teachers, come in a variety of forms. Guatama Buddha is considered to be one of the greatest ascended masters in the East.

Ascended masters

Ascended masters were usually teachers, gurus or spiritually enlightened people when they were living on this planet. They are spirits who have achieved "ascension" and offer themselves in service to humanity, not just to one individual. They include figures such as Jesus, the Virgin Mary, Buddha, Krishna, Abraham and master teachers such as White Eagle and Kwan Yin.

In the 19th century, Madame Blavatsky, one of the founders of the Theosophical Society, channelled messages from masters she called "mahatmas", who had lived in the Himalayas. Blavatsky's successors developed the idea of "ascended masters", and one of the best-known examples is Elizabethan philosopher Sir Francis Bacon, whose previous lives included Merlin and Christopher Columbus and who then ascended to become known as Master Rakozi.

A widely known channeller of spirit masters is J.Z. Knight, who claims to channel the spirit of Ramtha, a 30,000-year-old man. Other well-known channellers are Americans Jane Roberts for Seth, Esther Hicks for Abraham and Margaret McElroy for Maitreya.

Co-founder of the 19th-century esoteric Theosophical Society, Madame Helena Blavatsky was highly regarded in popular mediumship, and reported contact with many ascended beings including those from an obscure cult in the Himalayas.

Ancestral guides

An ancestral guide is one who can claim some sort of kinship with you, such as your grandfather who passed away when you were a child, or someone who has had some kind of relationship with your family further back in history. Many people view these types of guides as "guardians". Currently, there is a renewed spiritual interest in discovering one's family tree and ancestral history and the role we play out for all who have gone before us. By knowing about our family tree, we can make contact with specific ancestors, who can give us advice on our personal life journey. These beings are always watching over us and we are part of them as they are part of us.

Channelling

Considered to be the ability to contact spirit guides and act as a conduit for information, channelling can either be performed for others or purely on one's own behalf. However, channelling, as opposed to mediumship (see pages 248–51), is also a term that can imply that the individual has received information, whether in the form of an idea, a creative inspiration, solution or healing force, from the universal storehouse of knowledge rather than directly from the spirit. The channeller can also access information from the psychic world via deities, plants, animals and the landscape.

Role of the oracle

Channelling is a modern term for the practice in many ancient cultures of receiving messages from gods or spirits via oracles. The word "oracle" comes from the Latin word *orare* meaning "to speak". In Tibet, for example, the oracle is still important in religion and government. The Tibetan oracle, or *kuten,* is a spirit who enters specific individuals ito relay predictive messages. The Dalai Lama still consults the official oracle of the Government of Tibet in exile, an expert in trance-possession known as the Nechung Oracle.

Trance-channelling

In many indigenous tribal cultures, trance-channelling was performed by a shaman to travel to the spirit world. Trance-channelling was also used by mediums (although often charlatans) in the popularized parlour seances of the 19th century (see page 14). Modern shamans often use drums, spinning dances, meditation and vision quests to achieve a deeper state. Most channellers remain in an altered state of consciousness rather than an unconscious state. In a conscious state the channeller controls the communication pathway and can close the door at any time.

A shaman performs an ancient ritual dance in Tuva Siberia, Russia.

Channelling exercise

Before embarking on any channelling work, make sure you have practised the chakra-strengthening (see pages 98–9) and aura-nurturing exercises (see page 131). To leave the session at any time or to terminate any spiritual contact, stamp your feet several times on the floor before closing down the Light of Protection around you.

1 Enter your psychic sanctuary (see pages 100–1) and do the protection ritual on page 239.

2 Decide how long you want the session to take. If you are group-channelling with friends, begin the session by sitting in a circle, joining hands and reciting a prayer, affirmation or positive invocation. You can also sing a song together to evoke positive energy. Repeat a prayer of intention and a blessing for guidance and protection.

3 Invite your spirit guide to enter.

4 Keeping your intentions focused, ask basic questions to begin with, such as, "Are you male or female?", "What purpose do you serve in my life?", "What is your name?", "Are there any messages for me? Always be polite and thank the spirit for any answers, but do not let it take control. Do not ask the spirit to make your decisions for you and don't worry if nothing happens at first – keep trying.

5 If you are using automatic writing (see pages 208–11), don't worry about your style or grammar; let the writing flow spontaneously.

6 End punctually. Offer thanks to your spirit guides. Stamp on the floor twice to clear the energy. Now, gradually close down the Light of Protection around you by visualizing the golden light slowly being absorbed back into your body and then leaving through your Crown Chakra.

7 Return to ordinary consciousness. Eat a light meal, drink some tea or go for a walk to ground yourself.

Whirling dervishes in Istanbul perform as part of the Sema ceremony, in remembrance of God. Invoking a trance-like state to connect to the spiritual world, they channel positive universal energy through their mesmerizing spinning action.

Mediumship

Mediums provide the link between the spiritual and mundane worlds, channelling or mediating messages from the deceased of a loved one to the person still living. The main objective of a medium's work is to prove survival of the soul after death and to help the bereaved come to terms with their loss.

Mediums need to produce substantial information to satisfy the querent that their family member, friend or loved one still survives in the spirit world. This may be through accurate descriptions of the deceased, their work, personal anecdotes and the people they knew. Although a medium is usually psychic, people who call themselves "psychic" are not necessarily mediums. While many mediums have developed the powers of clairvoyance and prophecy, in some forms of spiritualism the medium is forbidden to make predictions and can only give information to prove there's life after death.

Controversy

The origin of mediumship is often linked to the three Fox Sisters, who were practising in 1848 in New York. Controversial forerunners of spiritualism, they were famed for their claim to be able to hear spiritual "rappings". The Scottish medium, Daniel Dunglas Home, who was renowned for his extraordinary levitation stunts, did much to make spiritualism fashionable among the aristocracy with his high-profile activities. However, many mediums practising at the time were exposed as so-called fakes by both the spiritualists and the Society for Psychical Research (see pages 15–16).

Mediumship in the 19th century gained popularity and respectability through the spiritualist movement. Followers of the Spiritualist Church also believe in God and Jesus Christ and merge religious belief with contact with the spirits of the dead. Mediums still thrive in the UK and US today.

Emma Hardinge Britten was an English-born spiritualist who became popular in America. She was a provocative and tireless promoter of the spiritualist movement.

The 19th-century Fox Sisters, Margaret, Kate and Leah, were considered pioneers of spiritualism and enjoyed success as mediums until 1888, when Margaret confessed that their "rappings" were a hoax. She recanted her confession, but their reputation was already ruined.

One of the principles of the US National Spiritualist Association of Churches is "Do unto others as you would have them do unto you." Trance-medium Emma Hardinge Britten conceived the seven fundamental precepts for the spiritualists. These are: the continuous existence of the human soul; personal responsibility; the fatherhood of God; the brotherhood of man; communion with spirits and angels; eternal compensation or retribution for good and evil deeds; and continual development open to every human soul.

Types of mediumship

Mental mediumship is the communication with spirits via telepathic means. The medium hears (clairaudience), sees (clairvoyance) and/or feels (clairsentience) messages from spirits. Directly, or with the help of a spirit guide, the medium passes the information on to the sitter – the person for whom the medium is doing a reading.

Trance-mediumship is where mediums remain in an alert but altered state of consciousness during a communication session. The spirit, or spirits, uses the medium as a channel and often speaks, chants or produces automatic writing. Leonora Piper was one of the most famous trance-mediums. Spirit guides who communicated through her include Martin Luther, Henry Longfellow, Abraham Lincoln and George Washington.

Physical mediumship may involve loud rappings and noises, materialized objects, spirit bodies and levitation. Most physical mediumship is presented in a darkened or dimly lit room, which is why it had so many associations with charlatans, and still does today, as it is far easier to fake results in poor light.

Colin Fry and Derek Acorah are two of the UK's best-known mediums.

Stanislawa Tomczyk (above) was a Polish medium renowned for her powers of telekinesis in the early 20th century.

Doris Stokes, popular UK psychic, was recognized as a clairaudient medium by the Spiritualists National Union in 1949. Her success created a resurgence of interest in psychic powers in the last part of the 20th century.

Spiritual questing and organized religion

According to US academic Robert Torrance in his book *The Spiritual Quest* (1994), the archetypal spiritual quest is an innate expression of our nature. The quest is not just a momentary mystical experience, but an ongoing expression of our most basic human drives.

The quest

Whether you long to travel the spiritual word as a shaman, find the answer to the creation of the universe as a scientist, call on the advice of spirits as a medium or simply wonder at infinity as a philosopher, you have the potential to quest for a personal spiritual truth. We may not be conscious of this quest, but it is dormant and waiting to be triggered by a rare moment of being "at one with the universe", a visit from a spirit, angel or apparition, or an intuition that there is a deeper meaning behind the veil of life.

Finding your path

Some form of psychological personal development is often thought to be needed before spiritual development can take place, but we can work at both pathways simultaneously and set out on our own spiritual quest, either within or without an organized belief system.

For many people a spiritual guru, such as the Indian-born Krishnamurti, may be enough. Others choose to read a spiritual questing book such as James Redfield's *The Celestine Prophecy* and Carlos Castenada's *Teachings of Don Juan*, based on the latter's initiation and profound awakening to spiritual experiences via a shamanic teacher, Don Juan Matus.

The vision quest

Among Native Americans, the "vision quest" involves a time of fasting under the guidance of a shaman, or is induced with the use of hallucinogenic plants. The quest is usually a journey alone in the wilderness to seek spiritual awakening from either a spirit guide, such as a power animal (see pages 240–1), or directly from the universal spirit, known by the Sioux, Dakota and Omaha peoples as "WakanTanka" or Great Mystery. Traditionally, the quester chooses a place far from human contact and sits inside a circle. In an altered state of consciousness, the quester then reaches an enlightened state via dreams or spiritual contact.

A Chimú Peruvian painted textile depicting cacti that produce a hallucinogenic sap used in vision-questing.

Sacred journeys and retreats

Retreat from the world in contemplation or meditation has been another way of seeking spiritual enlightenment and has been undertaken by many seekers worldwide, from the Buddha to various orders of monks and nuns.

You don't have to be religious, however, to take a sacred journey or go on a retreat. Many centres, such as the Findhorn Foundation in Scotland, encourage a global sense of spirituality, with no specific beliefs – the focus is more on each individual having their own spiritual experience. Pilgrimages or sacred journeys are also undertaken, usually in groups but also individually, to goddess shrines such as Tubtim, Bangkok; sacred landscapes such as Ayers

Rock in Australia; and religious mystery sites such as Turin (for the miraculous shroud), Garabandal in Spain (site of angelic apparitions) and the Christian pilgrimage trail to Santiago de Compostela in Spain, made famous more recently by actress and spiritual writer Shirley Maclaine.

Organized religion

Organized religion is practised by a large cultural group, the members of which often share the same traditions, customs, beliefs and spiritual goals. The word "religion" is rooted in the Indo-European word *leig*, meaning "to bind" or "to gather together". This model of religion offers us a way to sublimate our innate spiritual or divine longings. To find a way back to the source is, according to psychologist Carl Jung, a perennial human need. There are many diverse orthodox religious traditions worldwide.

The interfaith movement

Currently, religious bodies are becoming more open to a worldwide "interfaith" movement that encourages dialogue between different belief systems. This will allow for a more all-inclusive approach to spirituality, rather than the dominance of one religion over others or each religion's insistence that it is the true "way". Religion is a larger reflection of social and political values, saying, "You do not need to seek, for it is already found." However there are some who do not need to seek for themselves and are happy to accept the certainties offered by organized religion.

The Camino de Santiago de Compostela, also known as the Way of St James, has been walked by pilgrims for over 1,000 years. The medieval pilgrims believed that the Apostle James' remains were carried by boat from Jerusalem to northern Spain, where he was buried at the site of Santiago de Compostela. This picture shows a sculpture along the route.

Past lives

Have you ever felt that you might have been a famous person in a previous lifetime? Do you sometimes have flashes of memories that seem to be nothing to do with your own current life? Are you open to the idea of reincarnation – that you have lived other lives before and that you will again? The belief in reincarnation is the key concept of "past lives". Currently in psychological circles therapists conclude that an individual who has, or believes they have, experienced a previous life can use this experience to help them understand their purpose or role in this life.

Reincarnation

This is the belief that the essence, or soul, of the individual is born or incarnated again into the flesh of a different body and is the core of many religious traditions. In India, for example, both in its ancient Vedic traditions and more recent Hindu religion, reincarnation is an essential element of faith. Inuit and other Native American traditions, Sufism, Greek and Norse mythology, Buddhism and many modern-day spiritualities all embrace the idea that the essence of an individual incarnates into another human body after the death of the previous body. This essence can be referred to as the "soul" or "spirit" and can also be considered to be part of the "divine essence" or the Higher Self.

Depending on one's religious or cultural beliefs, the time between leaving one life and moving into the next varies. Most Christian and Islamic believers reject reincarnation as an idea, whereas many modern pagans, certain African traditions and followers of esoteric and mystical philosophies believe that the soul must pass through a spiritual level before it can travel between one life and the next.

Karma

Karma, or "action" in Sanskrit, means believing that how we act in one life has an influence in the next life. In contemporary spiritual language, the term "karma" has been popularized to mean that if, in a past life, you did "bad" things or thought "evil" thoughts, then in the next life you would pay the consequences. So in this life, if you are having a run of bad luck such as unemployment or a difficult relationship, then it's due to the karmic nature of your soul or the experiences or actions of the person you were in your last life. Now is your chance to make up for it. If, however, you were good, loved well and lived a fairly sinless life, then in this life you will receive the gift of a better life. Many celebrities believed themselves to have lived before. Henry Ford was convinced that he was a soldier killed at the battle of Gettysburg, while John Lennon believed that he was the reincarnation of Napoleon and Yoko Ono believed she was a reincarnation of Napoleon's wife, Josephine.

In Buddhism, the lotus symbolizes not only purity and faithfulness, but the cycle of the soul. From its previous incarnation – the depths of the pool – it is now in its current incarnation, this life, opening up toward total enlightenment, its next incarnation.

Past-life therapy

Some psychotherapists use past-life regression (PLR) to resolve emotional and psychological problems or to activate spiritual awakening. Many clients have past-life stories that reflect their current life problems. For example, a fear of commitment or attachment in intimate relationships in a current life is thought to be the result of serial betrayal in a past life. Thus PLR therapists claim that unresolved wounds from a past life (the soul's "karma") are responsible for present psychological problems.

In-between lives

Therapists also use hypnosis and visualization techniques to regress the individual to the place between two lives, in other words to reconnect to the soul, spirit or divine essence in the "inter-life". This is also called "spiritual regression". During the regression to their in-between life, subjects can review a past life assisted by spirit guides or evolved souls, plan their next life and choose past-life strengths to help them improve their current life.

Past-life reading

In past-life reading, the reader either focuses on one past life (one distinct period of time in that life) or they move through the years and decades, pausing to focus on important events. Unresolved emotional issues that are carried from one life to another can be seen as either a useful guide for living in this life or the very blockages that are holding the individual up on their present life journey.

Sensing a past life

If you answer "Yes" to most, or all, of these questions, then it is likely that
you are recalling some sense of a past life.

Y N
❑ ❑ Do you have an overwhelming desire to visit a certain place, but have no
        idea why?
❑ ❑ Are there any places you would never like to visit, but have no idea why?
❑ ❑ Do you ever experience déjà vu?
❑ ❑ Do you love reading about certain periods in history?
❑ ❑ Do you avoid reading about certain periods in history?
❑ ❑ Do you meet new people and think that perhaps you've met them in
        another life?
❑ ❑ Is there a city, area or country that you really identify with?

Ghosts and spirits

Ghosts are believed to be the spirits of dead people or animals who are still "earthbound" for various reasons. The ghost is thought to cling on to the material world, whether to a place, an object or even to another human being. Often, it is felt, ghosts and spirits don't even realize that their physical bodies are dead. While a ghost is believed to be the disembodied soul of a deceased entity who has not yet successfully crossed over, a spirit is thought to have made a successful transition to the afterlife. Spirits should never be mistaken for ghosts as they can visit the material world and return to the spiritual one at will, whereas a ghost remains in limbo.

It is believed that unresolved inner conflicts, feelings of revenge, guilt or a desperate need to finish some earthly business usually prevent ghosts from crossing over to the other side. Usually purported to be harmless, as they supposedly have no physical body, ghosts are nevertheless experienced as being quite frightening or, if they are not experienced, they are feared. Mediums are sometimes asked come to a supposedly haunted building to contact ghosts in order to help them to move on to the afterlife.

Research and speculation

"Pareidolia", an innate tendency to recognize patterns in random perceptions, is what some sceptics believe causes people to think that they have seen ghosts. Reports of ghosts "seen out of the corner of the eye" are thought to be due to the sensitivity of human peripheral vision. Some researchers, such as neuroscientist Michael Persinger, have speculated that changes in geomagnetic fields of the earth's crust, which also cause geomagnetic stress and are associated health issues, could stimulate the brain to produce many of the experiences of so-called haunting.

A representation of a successful ghost-hunter, seen in action during the 1950s, watching an apparition apparently walk through a solid wall.

Traditional beliefs

Apparitions have been under investigation by parapsychologists for over a century. From sightings of translucent glows, wispy whirls and even life-like human forms, the concept of "ghost" continues to prove enigmatic and elusive. In Ancient Greece ghosts were considered frightening spirits who could work for good or evil. The spirit of a dead person was believed to hover near the corpse's resting place and burial grounds were places to avoid. The dead were ritually mourned through ceremony, sacrifice and libations and ghosts would often return to haunt the families of the dead. The Ancient

The Day of the Dead is celebrated in Mexico in honour of souls who have passed on. Its origins date to an ancient Aztec festival.

Idols or papier mâché dolls are often burnt as offerings at the traditional Taoist Hungry Ghost Festival.

Greeks held annual feasts to honour and placate the spirits of the dead, after which the ghosts were told to leave until the same date the following year.

Western beliefs

In European popular culture, belief in ghosts was usually accompanied by the fear of "revenants"; spirits of the dead who returned to harm the living. Throughout the medieval and Renaissance periods, spirits, ghosts and demons intermingled with the living, but with the Age of Enlightenment, the spirit world became less feared and more derided.

Renewed interest

In the 19th century, the revival of spiritual ideas and occult practice encouraged renewed interest and belief in ghosts in popular culture. Since then extensive research has been carried out in the West by parapsychologists to try to prove whether ghosts exist or not. Hallowe'en, on October 31, is the evening before All Saints' Day in the Christian calendar. Devoted to ghosts and the supernatural, Hallowe'en aligns with a date that was important as the seasonal turning point of the pagan year (Samhain).

Eastern traditions

The ghost has traditionally been a popular, respected entity in Eastern traditions. For example, the worship of ancestral spirits plays a huge role in Chinese and Japanese cultures and many Chinese people believe it possible to contact the spirits of their ancestors through a medium, or that ancestors can help descendants if they are appropriately respected and rewarded. The annual ghost festival, which usually takes place in August, is celebrated by Chinese people around the world and is when ghosts and spirits of deceased ancestors are invited to participate in earthly celebration.

Haunting

This occurs wherever a ghost is perceived to be attached – whether to a building, a person, a street or a ship. Supernatural activity inside homes is mainly associated with tragic events that have occurred in the building's past. The place of haunting is usually thought to be of extreme importance to the ghost, as the earthly business that needs resolution is usually connected to the location.

Spirits and elementals

Spirits include all types of animal and human energies. Worldwide, the spirit world has been both a link to the dead, but also to other worlds. Elementals, fairies, goblins and land spirits are also thought to attach themselves to a place or person, but they have a more mischievous or darker, demonic energy. This energy has a different quality and is described in a range of ways

Types of haunting

Whether you are entering a supposedly haunted house or are spooked by what seems to be a ghostly apparition, you are experiencing one of two types of haunting.

RESIDUAL HAUNTING

According to parapsychologists, this is where an event has been captured in time, leaving a "spiritual footprint" or image. The event is experienced as a scene from a movie played over and over and is not interactive with the living. Although people may report seeing a ghost staring right at them or making some

kind of sign, it is believed that the ghost does not know that there is anyone there. The onlooker is seeing the residue of energy left over from the original event.

CLASSIC HAUNTING

Here, the ghostly presence includes all the sounds, visions, smells and feelings that interact with the living. Supernatural energies in a classic haunting are considered to be the ghost's way of getting human attention or seeking assistance, or even its desire to return to the physical world.

Churches, ruins and dark places are all considered rife with ghostly inhabitants. This is in part due to our ability to tune in to our psychic sense and peripheral vision in dim light, so we are able to "see" these apparitions or sense their presence.

– from "sparkling" in the case of fairies, to "dense" when describing goblins or elves. "Shadow people" are thought to be dark, vague humanoid shapes, usually seen in peripheral vision or the hypnagogic state – midway between being awake and asleep. They are rarely thought to intend or cause harm.

Poltergeists

These phenomena have recently been one of the most publicized types of spirit energy, but they remain the most misunderstood; they are not actually ghosts, nor are they connected with the spirit of someone who has passed on. Poltergeist activity is generally associated with children, adolescents and/or those with emotional problems. Though not completely understood, it is believed that the person is unconsciously creating psychokinetic activity in the form of loud bangings, electrical disturbances, moving furniture or levitating objects.

Angels

Making contact with a guardian angel is an appealing idea for those who either have a sense of religious roots or who just want to trust in the idea that a higher spirit of goodness, religious or pagan, is there to look after us. Using your psychic powers, you can learn to communicate with your soul's guide.

Angel history

The word "angel" comes from a Greek word meaning "messenger", which was simply a translation of a term for the messengers of God in the Hebrew Bible, and later the New Testament and the Qu'ran. Angels appear more frequently in the New Testament. Before Christianity "angels", or rather "messengers", appeared in Greek, Egyptian, Vedic and most world mythologies in one form or another. Guardian spirits or angels were also notable in Polynesian, Greek, Celtic and Native American myth.

Daniel was the first biblical character to refer to individual angels by name, but originally they were depicted without wings, so that the Christian Church could ensure that angels were not associated with the winged spirits of pagan beliefs – ironically their very source. By the 4th or 5th century, the Church had agreed on the different categories and hierarchies of angel, each with appropriate missions and activities. For example, some angels were thought to protect and guide humans; others merely carried out God's tasks. From around the 12th century the religious appeal of angels in Europe evolved into a populist embellishment in literature and art.

These days there is a revived interest in angels and, with the need for spiritual growth and disillusionment with orthodox religions, we are discovering that we can call on a guardian spirit who is not necessarily a Christianized angel but is more an angel protector and personal guide.

An illustration by William Blake from John Milton's epic poem *Paradise Lost*. The poem was concerned with the story of the fallen angels' attempt to take over heaven – a literary analogy for the 17th-century political uprising of Cromwell against the monarchy. The 18th-century visionary and poet Blake recorded seeing angels in trees as a young child.

Guardian angels

The guardian angel in Greek mythology and in Neoplatonic and occult traditions was known as a "daimon"; a word that also came to be used by the Greek translators of the Jewish Bible for any "evil" spirit, evolving into our present-day word "demon". According to the 3rd-century Greek Neoplatonists, Plotinus and Iamblichus, the daimon is our true guardian spirit, who accompanies our soul and guides us from birth to know our true calling and destiny.

Angel hierarchy

In the 4th or 5th century CE, the Greek mystic Dionysius the Areopagite divided the angels into nine orders, consisting of three choirs.

THE FIRST CHOIR

These three orders of angels are nearest to God, being dedicated to the face-to-face worship of God:

Seraphims are the closest of the angelic order to God, often known as the "burning ones" because they are aflame with love and devotion to God.

Cherubims, the name meaning "one who intercedes", have a protective role and are often depicted with large, winged animal bodies and human faces.

Thrones are shown as wheels of divine fire surrounding God's throne. They carry out God's decisions and are angels of justice.

THE SECOND CHOIR

These three orders of angels are dedicated to the knowledge of God through the universe:

Dominions bring wisdom and knowledge and are angels through whom God shows mercy.

Virtues show courage, earning them the name "the shining ones".

Powers work to keep fallen angels and devils from taking power over the universe.

THE THIRD CHOIR

These are known as "ministering angels", dedicated to caring for humans:

Principalities guard the world's nations.

Archangels are the chief angels, carrying God's messages to humans.

Angels are the lowest rank in the hierarchy, working as intermediaries between God and humans and between God and nature.

By developing your psychic powers you are more able to find your own personal guardian angel/daimon, rather than relying on orthodox named angels. Perhaps one of these famous angels has been there all along, guiding your soul's journey from life to life (see the box below for a brief list). If you feel a resonance with any of these names, they will be of importance to you. But these angels help and protect many others, too. The guardian angel you knew as a child, your fantasy or imaginary friend (if you can remember their name) may be the one you need to call on again.

Well-known angel names

If an angel's name resonates with you, then it may be of significance.

Camael Angel of Joy
Cathetel Angel of the Garden
Charoum Angel of Silence, inspiring us to be good listeners
Ecanus Angel of Writers
Elijah Angel of Innocence, believed to have created the Tree of Life
Hadraniel Angel of Love
Hael Angel of Kindness
Isda Angel of Nourishment
Liwet Angel of Inventions
Nisroc Angel of Freedom
Paschar Angel of Vision
Pistis Sophia Angel of Creation/Wisdom
Perpetiel Angel of Success
Raziel Angel of Mysteries
Samandiriel Angel of Imagination
Sofiel Angel of Nature
Uriel Angel of Creativity
Yofiel Angel of Divine Beauty
Zagzagel Angel of Wisdom

St Uriel, depicted here in a church window detail, means "God is my light" and is called upon to heal emotional wounds and offer forgiveness.

How to find your own guardian angel

Discovering your guardian angel is like meeting your soulmate: you instantly know that this entity will help you. This visualization will give you confidence to trust your psychic powers and listen to your angelic guide.

1 Find a quiet place to sit comfortably, where you won't be disturbed. Go to your psychic sanctuary (see pages 100–1).

2 Now visualize yourself in a beautiful walled garden. As you walk across the grass and past the sweet-smelling roses, you see a high wooden gate ahead of you. You cannot see what is on the other side, but you open the gate because you know you are going to meet someone who will look after you. If you remember the imaginary friend you had as a child, call for them now.

3 As you step out of the garden into the countryside, there are fields of lavender, forests and rolling hills in the distance. Above the hills is a rainbow, one end falling far beyond the horizon and the other only a few steps in front of you.

4 You walk toward the end of the rainbow and stand inside the spectrum of colours, which radiates throughout you. The colours permeate your Crown Chakra, then your whole being is filled with rainbow light. You aura is perfectly balanced and you feel at one with the universe.

5 Ask for your angel to appear to you. You want to know who they are.

6 You see, hear, touch or feel a figure bathed in the rainbow light, too. This is your chance to ask the angel's name. In your mind or out loud ask the angel and their name will come to you. It may be strange or very ordinary; it may be the name of your imaginary friend. After you have received the name, ask for signs in the coming weeks that this is truly your guardian angel.

7 Then thank the angel by name, leave the rainbow and return to the garden. Close the gate behind you and then close down your chakras (see page 102).

8 In the weeks to come, if you experience any synchronistic moments – meaningful coincidences of the angel's name in your day-to-day life – then consider this to be your personal angel. Never let anyone else know their name. From now on you can call on your personal guardian angel at any moment to guide you.

MEANINGFUL COINCIDENCES:

✳ You pick up a book in a shop and open it randomly. There on the page is the name of your angel or a symbol that you can associate with that name.

✳ You hear the name in someone else's conversation or you meet someone new with that name.

✳ If it's an unusual or foreign name, then you will be alerted to the symbol of that name. Perhaps if it's a name like Raiz, for example, one day you notice how the rays of the sun are always glinting in the trees. Use your imagination. Your imagination is the link to your psychic world, use it to work with and wonder at the signs around you and to enable your guardian angel to guide you in this life, too.

May the light of the universe shine through you every day.

Glossary

Akashic Records The records of everything that has ever happened on earth – believed to be found on the astral plane.

Altered state of consciousness A state of consciousness, such as hypnosis, trance or meditation, which is different to "normal" states of waking or sleeping.

Angel A benevolent spiritual being, usually bearing a message.

Ascended master A teacher-spirit who has once lived on earth.

Astral travel The ability to travel in the astral or spiritual planes.

Aura A vibrational field of electromagnetic energy surrounding and emanating from every living thing.

Automatic writing Writing that relays messages from the spirit world via your hand.

Ceromancy A divination method whereby melted wax is dripped into water to form patterns for interpretation.

Chakra Sanskrit word, meaning "wheel", which is an energy centre of the subtle body.

Channelling The ability to receive messages from the spiritual world or direct from the cosmic consciousness.

Clairaudience The power to receive spiritual messages via sounds not heard by the normal person.

Claircognizance The ability to know things without being told them.

Clairsentience The power of receiving information about people or things by feeling the energy surrounding the person or the object.

Clairvoyance To see or be aware of spiritual ideas or entities via the Third Eye or via visualization techniques.

Collective consciousness Another term for the cosmic storehouse of all knowledge.

Cosmic consciousness The total intelligence and power of all the universes.

Crystal ball A ball made of clear quartz crystal used for divination purposes to reveal information.

Déjà vu A French phrase, meaning "already seen", for the strange sensation of having been in exactly the same place or experiencing the same set of circumstances, as once before.

Dowsing A means of divination using a pendulum or rods to determine answers to questions, depending on the movement and vibrations of the tools used.

ESP Extra-sensory perception, also known as intuition and the sixth sense, is the ability to receive knowledge through other means than the five known senses.

Grounding A technique that helps you become down to earth and remain in touch with reality while you are performing psychic skills.

Guardian angel An angel, spirit or entity who looks after each individual from birth.

I Ching A divinational system of 64 hexagrams developed in ancient Taoist philosophy and used as an oracle.

Kirlian photography A means of revealing the colours and range of the human aura.

Lucid dreaming The state of being aware that you are dreaming, even though you are still asleep.

Medium A psychic person who contacts the spirit of the deceased to give assurance that the deceased person is happy and safe in the afterlife. They also relay messages to the living.

NDE Near-death experience, in which people claim to have seen angels, visions, white light or the spiritual world at a moment very close to death.

OBE An out-of-body experience, which is described as leaving the body and viewing it from another place.

Oracle A place, object or person through whom a deity or a spiritual force is believed to speak and reveal hidden knowledge.

Precognition Knowing something before it actually happens.

Premonition A sensation, usually not welcome, of something that will happen in the future.

Psyche The soul, spirit or, in contemporary psychology, the mind.

Psychokinesis The ability to move physical objects by a psychic means other than through the five known senses.

Seance A group meeting for those who want to contact spiritual beings.

Sixth sense Also known as ESP (extra-sensory perception) and intuition, the sixth sense is our ability to contact the spiritual world through means other than the usual five senses.

Spirit guide An entity from the spirit world who both guides and gives advice or information to a person who is psychic.

Synchronicity A meaningful coincidence or set of events that share the same symbolic features and give personal meaning for an individual.

Reincarnation The soul or spirit reborn into another life or new physical body.

Remote viewing An ability to psychically "see" what is happening in any part of the world from another place.

Scrying A divination technique using the surface of reflective water, a mirror or a crystal ball to view and interpret shapes and patterns.

Symbol A manifest sign of something occult, mystical or hidden.

Tarot A deck of 78 mystical cards, which are a pathway to spiritual knowledge.

Telepathy The ability to send and receive information, whether as ideas, words or images, to another person via the psychic sense.

Third Eye A chakra centre of energy located above the eyes, usually mid-forehead, where we can channel psychic power both to receive information and to relay it.

Unworldly Not of this world; concerned with the spirit, soul and other universal planes of existence.

Zener cards A set of cards specially designed to aid telepathy.

Index

Picture acknowledgments

The publisher would like to thank the following people, museums and photographic libraries for permission to reproduce their material. Every care has been taken to trace copyright holders. However, if we have omitted anyone we apologize and will, if informed, make corrections to any future edition.

Key
AA The Art Archive; **BAL** The Bridgeman Art Library; **Getty** Getty Images
l = left, r = right, a = above, b = below

Page 1 JLP/Deimos/Corbis; **2** DAJ/Getty; **7** Fototeca Storica Nazionale/Getty; **8** Marnie Burkhart/Corbis; **10** UniversalImagesGroup/Hulton Archive/Getty; **13** Art Gallery of South Australia, Adelaide/Gift of the Rt. Honourable, the Earl of Kintore 1893/BAL; **14** Mary Evans Picture Library; **16** Harry Price/Mary Evans Picture Library; **17** Mary Evans Picture Library; **19(l)** Phototake/Alamy; **19(r)** Manfred Kage/Getty; **20** Jerry Cooke/Time & Life Pictures/Getty; **21** Interfoto/Alamy; **22** Victorian Card/Mary Evans Picture Library; **25** Sigmund Freud copyrights/Mary Evans Picture Library; **27** Hemis.fr/SuperStock; **29** Jules Selmes/Duncan Baird Publishers; **30** Charles Walker/TopFoto; **33** Museum of Fine Arts, Boston, Massachusetts/Denman Waldo Ross Collection/BAL; **36–7** Stephen Flint/Alamy; **40–41** ZenShui/Alix Minde/Getty; **43** Central Press/Hulton Archive/Getty; **44** Malcolm Schuyl/Alamy; **46** Amazon-Images/Alamy; **49** Hank Morgan/Science Photo Library; **50–51** Dale O'Dell/Alamy; **52–3** Imagebroker/Alamy; **55** Peter Barritt/Alamy; **56–7** Ivan Kmit/Alamy; **59** Viv Yeo/Narratives/Photolibrary; **60–61** Phototake Inc./Alamy; **63** Bettmann/Corbis; **64–5** Arco Images GmbH/Alamy; **66–7** David Noton Photography/Alamy; **69** Elizabeth Etienne/Alamy; **70** ImageState/Alamy; **73** ZenShui/Alix Minde/Getty; **74–5** Lorie Leigh Lawrence/Alamy; **76** The Art of Tarot Cards, Dover Publications; **78** Nic Cleave/Alamy; **79** Alexander Sandvoss/Alamy; **80–81** Jules Selmes/Duncan Baird Publishers; **82** Andy Crawford/Dorling Kindersley/Getty; **83** Age Fotostock/SuperStock; **85** Mika/Corbis; **86** Stockbyte/Getty; **88** i love images/Alamy; **89** Michele Constantini/PhotoAlto/Corbis; **93** Photolibrary/Getty; **95** The Wellcome Library, London; **98–9** David R. Frazier/Photolibrary/Alamy; **101** Tom Mackie/Alamy; **102** Michael Freeman/Corbis; **105** Emilio Ereza/Alamy; **106** Momentimages/Getty; **109** Ocean/Corbis; **110** CVI Textures/Alamy; **112–13** Skyscan Photolibrary/Alamy; **114** Bettmann/Corbis; **115** Science Photo Library/Alamy; **116(a)** Caro/Alamy; **116(bl)** Phototake Inc./Alamy; **116(br)** Chico Sanchez/Alamy; **121** Bob Thomas/Getty; **125** Heide Benser/Corbis; **126** PhotoAlto/Alamy; **127** Sally Cornwell/Alamy; **131** Emotive Images/Alamy; **133** John James/Alamy; **134** ImageZoo/Alamy; **137(l)** Interfoto/Mary Evans Picture Library; **137(r)** Interfoto/Mary Evans Picture Library; **138** Altrendo images/Getty; **141** Renate Forster/STOCK4B/Getty; **142** Science and Society/Getty; **143** Private Collection/Christie's Images/BAL; **145** Carl Pendle/Alamy; **146** Sanna Pudas/Getty; **149** Private collection/Nativestock Pictures/BAL; **150–51** Kip Evans/Alamy; **152–3** David Noton Photography/Alamy; **155** British Library/AA/Alamy;

157 Marc Charmet/Bibliothèque Nationale Paris/AA; **161** Parav Sahni/Alamy; **162** Richard Sheppard/Alamy; **166** Photolibrary/Getty; **169** Marc Charmet/Private Collection/AA ; **172–7** The Art of Tarot Cards, Dover Publications; **185** Michaela Stejskalova/Alamy; **186** Corbis Cusp/Alamy; **188** Science Photo Library/Alamy; **190–92** Matthew Ward/Duncan Baird Publishers; **194** Per-Olof Andersson/iStockphoto; **195** Manuel Velasco/iStockphoto; **197–9** John Bigl/iStockphoto; **199** Glow Asia/SuperStock; **201(l)** Keren Su/Getty; **201(r)** Charles Taylor/Shutterstock; **202** Martyn Vickery/ Alamy; **208** SPR/Mary Evans Picture Library; **209** AA/Alamy; **212** Graham Ian Stebbings/Alamy; **215** Borderlands/Alamy; **217** Ilya Naymushin/Reuters/Corbis; **221** Hulton Archive/Getty; **222** Christoph Wilhelm/Getty; **225** Photolibrary/Getty; **227** Ace Stock Limited/Alamy; **229** Chad Ehlers/ Alamy; **230–31** Stocktrek Images, Inc/Alamy; **233** Egyptian Museum Cairo/Collection Dagli Orti/ AA; **235** Martin Lladó/Gaia Moments/Alamy; **236–7** Tara Urbach/Shutterstock; **239** Superstock/ Getty; **241** Peter Wey/Alamy; **242** Kentoh/Shutterstock; **243** Harry Price/Mary Evans Picture Library; **245** Images & Stories/Alamy; **247** Art Kowalsky/Alamy; **249(l)** Mary Evans Picture Library; **249 (r)** Mary Evans Picture Library; **250(l)** Louis Quail/In Pictures/Corbis; **250(r)** Peter Dench/In Pictures/ Corbis; **251(a)** Mary Evans Picture Library; **251(b)** Hulton Archive/Getty; **253** Private Collection/ Werner Forman Archive; **254** Cro Magnon/Alamy; **257** John Warburton-Lee Photography/Alamy; **259** Banana Pancake/Alamy; **261** Mary Evans Picture Library; **262(l)** Travis Houston/Shutterstock; **262(r)** JCREATION/Shutterstock; **265** The Marsden Archive/BAL; **267** Fitzwilliam Museum, University of Cambridge/BAL; **269** Stan Pritchard/Alamy.

Author acknowledgments

A big thankyou to everyone on the team (Bob Saxton, Sandra Rigby, Fiona Robertson, Jo Godfrey Wood, Peggy Sadler and Emma Copestake). Thanks also to my agent, Chelsey Fox, for the many years we've known each other; my family and friends for their support, belief and wisdom; and all the stars in the sky for being there.